PRAISE FOR *NAKED AND UNASHAMED*

"Refreshingly frank and direct in its guidance, *Naked and Unashamed* sketches out the field of Godly marriage realistically, but also includes the relational fences that safeguard couples. Root, Root, and Rios disenchant us with fairy tales to reenchant us with vulnerability, wonder, sex, communication, and more—things that make marriage and family sustainable. This compelling read will be my book of choice for the next round of pre-marital counseling!"

—**Dru Johnson, PhD**, Associate Professor of Biblical &
Theological Studies, The King's College, New York

"This is not just a book for those contemplating marriage, it's for all of us, no matter how many years we have been married. I recommend two copies, one for yourself and one for a couple that you know needs this critical Biblical perspective."

—**Dr. Erwin W. Lutzer**, Pastor Emeritus, The Moody Church, Chicago

"This book is a treasure trove of insight that comes from many years of learning to love each other and show the mystery of Christ and the church in a marriage. This honest, theologically driven, realistic guide on the way to the altar will go a long way in preparing those wanting to keep their sacred vows and love one another as long as they both shall live."

—**Erik Thoennes**, Chair, Department of Undergraduate Theological
Studies, Talbot School of Theology/Biola University; Pastor,
Grace Evangelical Free Church of La Mirada, CA

"I have performed scores of weddings over the years, and my wife and I have done the pre-marital counseling. I wish this insightful book had been available for us."

—**Lyle W. Dorsett, PhD**, Billy Graham Professor of
Evangelism, Beeson Divinity School

"Beth and I are just one of hundreds of couples that have been blessed to begin our marriage journey together with Claudia and Jerry Root, and the sweet delight of our nearly thirty years of marriage owes much to that first push in the right direction we received from our time with them. Learning to be truly intimate—to dare the hard work of sharing stories, hearts, minds, dreams, aspirations, and, lastly, bodies—is the long road of marriage. This book is a reliable map to that road."

—**The Very Revd Chip Edgar**, Dean and Rector of the Anglican Cathedral Church of the Apostles in Columbia, SC

"My wife and I have spent four decades doing pre-marital and marital counseling. I wish we'd had this book when we began. Jerry and Claudia Root's insights come from a lifetime of scholarship, pastoral care coupled with their experiences of living faithfully in the covenant of their own marriage. The insights found in *Naked and Unashamed* are, in a word, invaluable. We will definitely be using this book in future pre-marital counseling."

—**Pastor Reed and Lisa Jolley**, Santa Barbara Community Church

"I have known Jerry and Claudia Root for many years, and there is no one I would trust more to help couples understand what a strong and healthy and God-honoring marriage requires. I am acutely aware of the need for practical wisdom to help prepare couples for the lifelong journey of marriage, and that is precisely what they have given us. I can't wait to put this book into practice in our church!"

—**Jeff Frazier**, Lead Pastor, Chapelstreet Church, Geneva, IL

NAKED and
UNASHAMED

a guide to the necessary work
of Christian marriage

DR. JERRY ROOT
CLAUDIA ROOT & JEREMY RIOS

PARACLETE PRESS
BREWSTER, MASSACHUSETTS

*We'd like to dedicate this book to the more than 1500 couples
who have been, rather ludicrously, prepared for marriage
with this material over the past 30 years.*

*May the God who allowed His son to take crumbs and satisfy a
multitude, take these crumbs and bless multitudes again.*

2018 First Printing

Naked and Unashamed: A Guide to the Necessary Work of Christian Marriage

Copyright © 2018 by Gerald Richard Root, Claudia Ann Root, and Jeremy Michael Rios

ISBN 978-1-64060-065-2

Library of Congress Cataloging-in-Publication Data

Names: Root, Jerry, author.
Title: Naked and unashamed : a guide to the necessary work of Christian
marriage / Dr. Jerry Root, Claudia Root, and Jeremy Rios.
Description: Brewster, MA : Paraclete Press, Inc., 2018.
Identifiers: LCCN 2018005597 | ISBN 9781640600652 (trade paper)
Subjects: LCSH: Marriage--Religious aspects--Christianity.
Classification: LCC BV835 .R64 2018 | DDC 248.8/44--dc23
LC record available at https://lccn.loc.gov/2018005597

10 9 8 7 6 5 4 3 2 1

Published by Paraclete Press
Brewster, Massachusetts
www.paracletepress.com

Printed in the United States of America

CONTENTS

PREFACE: The Purpose of This Book   vii

Some Preliminary Guidelines for Engaged Couples   ix

CHAPTER 1: The Necessary Work   1

PART 1: **Undressing for Intimacy**   17

  CHAPTER 2: Undressing Your Stories   18

  CHAPTER 3: Undressing the Heart   28

  CHAPTER 4: Undressing the Mind   38

  CHAPTER 5: Undressing the Soul   48

PART 2: **Unpacking Communication**   63

  CHAPTER 6: Unpacking Gender   64

  CHAPTER 7: Unpacking Communication   80

  CHAPTER 8: Unpacking Woundedness   100

PART 3: **Exploring Expectations**   123

  CHAPTER 9: Exploring the Expectations of
      Family and Culture   124

  CHAPTER 10: Exploring the Expectations of
      Parenthood   136

  CHAPTER 11: Exploring Financial Expectations   148

PART 4: **Undressing for Sex**   159

  CHAPTER 12: Undressing the Sexual Self   160

  CHAPTER 13: Undressing for a Life of Sex   180

  CHAPTER 14: Undressing for the Wedding Night   192

PART 5: **Final Words**   199

  CHAPTER 15: On the Writing of This Book   200

  A SELECTED BIBLIOGRAPHY OF MARRIAGE HELPS   205

ACKNOWLEDGMENTS   207

NOTES   209

The Purpose of This Book

*T*his book exists because, despite the abundance of magazines, articles, and self-help volumes available, people continue to struggle with marriage.

On the one hand, the cottage industry of wedding planners, consultants, Pinterest pages, and independent bloggers has shaped young hearts to dream and plan for the biggest day of their lives. The day is everything, and they will plan each element with precision, from flowers to cake decorations to party favors. Acting on this crafted desire, couples will spend an enormous amount of time and money preparing for the wedding. Ironically, they will spend little to no time or money in preparation for their marriage itself. The investment into the perfect day is all out of proportion with the investment into life together *after* the day. At times it even seems as if people are more interested in *getting* married than they are in *staying* married. This book exists to help couples prepare for the rest of their life together.

On the other hand, it seems that too few couples comprehend the degree of work required to make a marriage successful. Divorce rates are clear evidence of this, but so also are the many married people who are in dire need of counseling and care, who persist in loneliness and difficulty, feeling ill-equipped to navigate the unforeseen difficulties of marriage. Many people hope one day to get married; few people seem to know what it really means to *be* married. The truth of the matter is that happy marriages rarely just happen. In fact, the majority of the time they will require at least as much energy and preparation as is directed toward the grand celebration on the wedding day. This book exists to coach couples through strategies that will assist them to succeed.

On the wedding day, a bride and groom will make a promise before God and the witness of their friends and family—a promise to have and hold one another, in sickness and health, in wealth or poverty, until death. Sometimes these promises are uttered in a rush of devoted emotion; at the same time sometimes their demands are glibly considered; yet no couple (we trust!) sets out intentionally to fail. While no book can promise perfect success, the best we can do—and this we hope to do—is to offer hope and guidance to couples in preparation for marriage, to couples struggling in marriage, and possibly encouragement to couples thriving in marriage. Marriage, in point of fact, is a living, growing thing, and a resource such as this one hopes simply to provide a plumb to what is bent, a balm to what is broken, and an enrichment to what is thriving.

If marriage is so difficult, and if the risks are so high, then it might be tempting to conclude that it is not worth bothering about. This is unsatisfying, chiefly because we are convinced that marriage—with all its difficulties—remains one of the best hopes for human happiness and fulfillment. A successful marriage is a thing of unprecedented and radiant beauty, and as G. K. Chesterton (a great believer in marriage) said, "If a thing is worth doing, it is worth doing badly."[1] This book is targeted for any person who wishes, given the liabilities of marriage, to attempt to maximize its benefits and experience the fullness of its joys.

Billy Bray, Welsh preacher and evangelist, hearing once about other people's trials of faith stood and exclaimed, "Well, friends, I have been taking vinegar and honey, but, praise the Lord, I've had the vinegar with a *spoon*, and the honey with a *ladle*."[2] Many couples may feel that in marriage they've had honey by the teaspoon and vinegar by the ladle. As we said, no book can promise success, and yet the couple that commits to reading together, to learning together, to discussing together, to developing good habits together—that couple will gain a significant advantage in the management and enjoyment of their common life. All marriages ought to begin with the best possible foundation. All existing marriages ought to have the courage to reexamine and correct their foundation as necessary. And, by God's grace, the honey will outweigh the vinegar beyond measure.

SOME PRELIMINARY GUIDELINES
FOR ENGAGED COUPLES

If you are an engaged couple reading this book, then there are six things we would like to say to you at the start.

1) It is critical that you devote regular time to the development of your relationship with your future spouse. You must not allow wedding plans to dominate your time together. Set aside time to invest in your marriage, especially if you plan for it to last longer than the wedding day.

2) Not only must you dedicate time, but you must commit—mutually—to engaging in the material. Where there are questions or exercises, do them. Where there are conversations to have, have them. If you find yourself incapable of divulging your life to this person through the contents of this book, you might think twice about committing to live with that person for the rest of your life.

3) If you are engaging in sex before marriage you are actively short-circuiting the process of intimacy in your relationship. If you are incapable of showing restraint before marriage, what makes you think you will have restraint within marriage? If you are disobeying God's voice before marriage, why do you think you will be able to discern Him properly? Premarital sexual conduct corrupts your capacity to make wise decisions, and your wedding is the biggest decision of your life. Show restraint, and begin your marriage upon a foundation of wisdom.

4) If you are living together, you should know that statistically this *increases* your chances for divorce. The commitment that marriage requires of you is not casual, and cohabitation before marriage encourages an attitude of non-commitment between couples. In other words, the bonds you forge by living together before marriage weaken the bonds you are intended to form *within* marriage. If you are living together at the time of reading, make a plan to live apart until your wedding day.

5) Unless you wish to conceive children immediately, now is the time to educate yourself with regard to the operations of pregnancy. Different traditions have different beliefs regarding birth control, so make sure you've discussed these issues together, with your clergy as appropriate, and with your physician if necessary. The important thing to remember is that the wedding night is not a good time to be making these kinds of plans, so make sure you've thought ahead.

6) Please work through the book in order, because there is an intentional progression to the intimacy discussed here. Furthermore, if you as a couple or an individual are tempted to skip ahead to the chapters on sex (you know who you are!), don't.

CHAPTER 1

The Necessary Work

Grow old along with me!
The best is yet to be.
—Robert Browning

THE FAIRY TALE

A few years ago the world watched enrapt as Prince William and his bride Kate Middleton spoke their vows before the Archbishop of Canterbury. Their story—the prince who falls in love with a common girl—is the very substance of fairy tales. The extravagance of their event—from horses to plate ware—was the stuff of Disney. One friend of mine even woke up at 3:00 AM, got a hat out of her closet, thawed a scone, brewed a cup of tea, and watched the wedding. Why would she do that? Because we love—we crave—fairy tales, and silently we wish that they would be true for us.

It is unlikely that any who read this book will be married by an archbishop, and few will be wed in a venue as magnificent as Westminster Abbey. Princes are rare these days. But on a wedding day, no matter how small or seemingly insignificant, a group of families and friends will gather to witness a fairy tale no less marvelous than the one people inconvenienced themselves to see some years ago. On their wedding day a boy and a girl make a promise in the presence of God and witnesses. It is a moment that is, for all involved, a miracle of vast and indescribable proportions. On your wedding day you solemnize the fairy tale that God is working in your lives.

On their wedding day, a bride and groom stand to mark the beginning of their marriage. They are saying, in the presence of God, "I am going to write the story of the rest of my life with you." Nobody there will know the ending of the story. Nobody can predict the dangers and turns a couple must face. Whether the couple's fairy tale has a happy ending or a sad one is their decision, and their work. And as with all fairy tales, it is the end of the story that gives meaning to the events within them.

As a matter of fact, there is one immutable fact about fairy tales: there are always trials to be gone through—a forest to cross, a wolf to defeat, an enemy to kill. Take the trial—the necessary work—out of the fairy tale and you no longer have a fairy tale. "Once upon a time there was a girl named Little Red Riding Hood who took food to her sick grandmother and came back home for tea." This doesn't make a good fairy tale at all. But the necessary trials of the fairy tale—the forest, the fearsome wolf, the huntsman—are given meaning and significance by its ending. It is only when the story is over, only when we look back, that we call it a good story; never before.

Perhaps some images can assist us to better understand this necessary work. Many people dream about purchasing a house, which they will turn into a home. In anticipation they invest time and energy into thinking about what kind of place they'd like to have someday—maybe they make lists of the kinds of characteristics they'd like it to have, its size, shape, number of rooms, the kinds of memories they'd like to have there. Then they shop together for this dream home. After the search—whether long or short—they finally find the home they want. And they purchase their perfect home and move into it, filling it with their things.

A successful homeowner inherits many responsibilities; there are chores to be done, gardens to be tended, window sashes to be painted, garbage to be taken out, roofs to be repaired, pipes to be plumbed, wiring to be watched over, and an untold number of details to be managed. But imagine with me if, after moving into this dream home, the couple fails to maintain it. Imagine that they never take the time to mow the lawn. After a couple of weeks the neighbors might politely remind them that, in this neighborhood, it's a tradition to cut your grass. Let a few more weeks go by and the neighbors will grow less friendly in their reminders, suggesting to you that if you won't mow your lawn, would you at least consider harvesting it? Imagine never keeping up on any of the maintenance of the house—if the drains get stopped up and you never clear them; if the wiring frays but you don't repair it; or as the roof deteriorates you don't replace it, but place strategic buckets along the corridors and in the bedrooms. Imagine the yard resembling the set of a Tarzan movie. Imagine the plaster falling off the walls, wallpaper peeling, mold and other fungi growing in the corners and recesses.

What has happened to the dream home? That couple spent so much time making the perfect choice—and now their dream home is a dilapidated remnant.

Consider also the glorious leaves of autumn, especially as they display themselves in the Midwestern and Eastern United States—trees set aflame with burning red, trees with yellow to rival the sun, and all the colors in between as well—oranges, russets, salmon, shrimp, maroons, peach, and auburn. But not long after this glorious display, these same leaves, now simply brown, are scattered everywhere and become a terrible, brown mess. Next time this happens go for a walk together, and pay attention especially for a yard, in the midst of all the others, that has no leaves at all—one that has been raked clean. When you come across that I think you'll find that there's something breathtaking about that sight; what is more, it didn't just *happen*.

Now, consider as well an elderly couple, still in love. Helmut Thielicke, German theologian and pastor, once observed such a couple who, after many years of marriage, still had a light in their eyes for one another. He observed them both carefully, noting the tenderness in their expressions toward one another. This intrigued him, and since he had known the couple for many years he was well aware of the authenticity of their love. It wasn't until he had left their home that he realized a truth: this couple had the marriage they deserved. His mind went to Genesis 2, where Adam declares that Eve is "bone of my bone, and flesh of my flesh." Adam might as easily have said, "this is boredom of my boredom, lovelessness of my lovelessness."[3] The choice therefore belongs to each couple precisely *what kind* of marriage they are going to have, and in view of this a man and woman can choose to say to one another, "This is now wonder of my wonder, fascination of my fascination, delight of my delight." What we put into marriage is in a very real way precisely what we get out of it. Maybe you'll encounter such a couple one day—gray hairs and wrinkled hands and paper-thin skin stretched across bony joints; but they are together, and you will note that their affection represents a lifetime of work on their relationship. Their love is also breathtaking. It didn't just *happen*. They *did something* to make their love possible.

The fairy tale home, the fairy tale yard, and the fairy tale marriage—none of these things just happen. And in all three stories, people performed the necessary work that brought meaning to the labor, the trial, the effort involved. We judge a story good by its conclusion, and so also a marriage.

ACKNOWLEDGING THE WORK

The kind and quantity of work necessary to create a successful marriage is deceptive. English gardens, some of which are hundreds of years old, are rightly famous for their beauty, and people travel from around the world to visit them. And yet their beauty is enormously deceptive; what presents itself to the eye appears natural—even spontaneous—when in fact it is attributable to the vigilant attention of the master gardener and his array of tools, fertilizers, schedules, and planning, and especially to his in-depth knowledge of plant life and the seasons. Similarly, great marriages present themselves to the outward eye as images of simplicity and beauty, but behind them lies an ongoing work, as well as an entire toolshed of skills and knowhow. Great marriages, like great gardens, never just happen.

The truth of the matter is that it is somewhat ludicrous to attempt to prepare anyone for marriage. When you learn to ride a bike, your technical knowledge of the assembly, composition, and individual parts of the bicycle—while not unimportant—is irrelevant when it comes to learning balance. In a similar way, marriage itself is the only true preparation for marriage. And this is one of the key reasons why *commitment* is so terribly important. The work required from you in marriage will exceed what you believe are your personal capacities, and therefore couples make a mutual promise before God that they will stick to one another no matter what. It is this promise, more than anything else, that makes marriages what they are. It is the trellis on which grows the intertwining vine of a couple's life and love.

We see this interaction when the Bible speaks of marital love in the *Song of Solomon*, where the image of a garden plays repeatedly.[4] The garden in the ancient world was another image of *paradise*—a walled and protected space dedicated to both pleasure and beauty. The biblical author of the Song perceives the cultivated space of a marriage in those same terms—a walled and protected space for husband and wife to enjoy pleasure and beauty. The walls are formed by commitment; the pleasure is grounded in intimacy.

And once again we should note the false commitment promised by sex before marriage. It is fundamentally a transgression because it *transgresses* the boundary of the garden before the right of access has been granted. It deceives the couple because it generates the *illusion* of commitment—by enjoying the benefits of the committed—prior to the *declaration* of commitment. Sexual intimacy has its rightful place within the committed relationship—it is an activity for the garden.

THE ORIGIN AND CALL OF MARRIAGE

Is it not noteworthy that the first marriage, of Adam and Eve, takes place within a garden paradise? Genesis 2:18–25 records their first encounter with one another:

> Then the LORD God said, "It is not good for the man to be alone; I will make him a helper suitable for him." Out of the ground the LORD God formed every beast of the field and every bird of the sky, and brought them to the man to see what he would call them; and whatever the man called a

living creature, that was its name. The man gave names to
all the cattle, and to the birds of the sky, and to every beast
of the field, but for Adam there was not found a helper suitable for him. So the LORD God caused a deep sleep to fall
upon the man, and he slept; then He took one of his ribs and
closed up the flesh at that place. The LORD God fashioned
into a woman the rib which He had taken from the man, and
brought her to the man.

The man said,
"This is now bone of my bones,
And flesh of my flesh;
She shall be called Woman,
Because she was taken out of Man."

For this reason a man shall leave his father and his mother, and
be joined to his wife; and they shall become one flesh. And the
man and his wife were both naked and were not ashamed.

God has created the world, and at the end of each day of creation
He has declared it "good." Five days are declared good, and on the
sixth, looking back over all, He says it is "Very good." But suddenly in
Genesis 2 something changes, and we discover that it is "not good" for
the man to be alone. The world as God has made it is very good, but it
is not complete. Our loneliness is not God's plan for humanity. We are
created for relationships.

This, at least in part, is one of the lessons from the naming of the
animals. Adam witnesses this lengthy parade of creatures moving past.
He sees Mr. and Mrs. Dog, and Mr. and Mrs. Elephant, and Mr. and
Mrs. Lion, and he begins to take note that each animal has a counter-
part, but not him. Furthermore, Adam discovers in his work that work
itself will not satisfy him. The job itself becomes an occasion for longing. It is easy to imagine that some of the animals become especially
companionable, such as the dog or the horse. But even they are not *like*
him. In this experience Adam's longing is awakened.

Made aware of his loneliness, God puts Adam to sleep, takes Eve from his side, and fashions her into a new creature. When Adam awakens, and sees her for the first time, his first words—the first recorded speech of mankind in the Bible—are poetry. "This is now bone of my bone, and flesh of my flesh, she shall be called woman, for she was taken out of man." In Hebrew the word used for man here is *Ish*, while the word used for woman is *Ishah*. Go ahead and recite those two words aloud right now. Roll them around your tongue and let them fall upon the ear. *Ish. Ishah.* Like me, but different.

Eve, we are told, is created as a "helpmeet" for Adam—not a slave, nor a servant, nor an employee, but a helpmeet. A companion in life and in work. Mike Mason in his book *The Mystery of Marriage* illuminates Eve's unique role in this story:

> The Lord God made woman out of a part of man's side and closed up the place with flesh, but in marriage He reopens this empty, aching place in man and begins the process of putting woman back again, if not literally in the side, then certainly at it: permanently there, intrusively there, a sudden lifelong resident of a space which until that point the man will have considered to be his own private territory, even his own body. But in marriage he will cleave to the woman, and the woman to him, the way his own flesh cleaves to his own bones.[5]

Marriage is the chosen, but discomfortingly forceful, encounter between a man and a woman. It is in fact the very design of marriage to answer our innate loneliness with a form of profound discomfort. We experience in marriage a closeness that we are designed to undergo, and yet one that we are not adept at accomplishing.

For people unaccustomed to sharing a bed with another human being, the first months of marriage can be quite challenging. Somehow, the number of elbows in the bed seems to increase beyond the simple math of 2+2. When Liesel and Jeremy were first married, not a few months into their marriage Liesel contracted a painful sinus infection. Her upper cheeks and face were swollen and incredibly tender.

Sometime during the night, rolling over in his sleep, Jeremy turned and elbowed her right in the face. Liesel wept, and Jeremy felt horrible—like some kind of abuser!—and apologized profusely. But several months later, when they were far more accustomed to sharing a bed, the same thing happened again. Liesel with a sinus infection, Jeremy rolling in his sleep—bam! Right in the face. Liesel, again, burst into tears, but this time Jeremy announced, "Well, that's marriage!" And promptly rolled back over and fell asleep.

Intimacy, like elbows in the bed, involves a closeness with which we are simply not familiar. And in fact, more than being unfamiliar with it, the intimacy asked of us in marriage strikes directly at our innermost selfishness. George MacDonald has said that "The one principle of hell is: I am my own."[6] The attitude of the unredeemed human heart is one of self-governance, self-determination, and self-preservation. I make all choices for me and for my own ends. But marriages cannot survive when partners live this ethic, and nothing quite like marriage will expose that selfishness in all its ugliness. Marriage, in fact, is very like a mirror in which my spouse reflects back at me all that is ugly about myself—my greed, my pettiness, my foolishness, my anger, my unforgiveness. Marriage in this respect is a school of selfishness.

The mirror operates in a way very like something Paul says in Romans 3:23, "For all have sinned and fall short of the glory of God." When we fall in love with our partner, the mirror reflects back to us all the good that we wish we could be. But in the course of commitment we discover what a great distance we must still go if we would truly become that person. In love, we see the glory; in living together, we fall short. Often this falling short creates despair—and I would suggest that a vast number of couples who turn to divorce do so simply because of this disparity. Not liking who they see in the mirror with their spouse, they opt to change spouses. What they fail to acknowledge is that the ugly image they came to despise was their own.

THE CONFLICT OF CLOSENESS

For couples who persist in their commitment, however, the gap between the person we wish we were, and the person we really are, often generates conflict. There are disappointed expectations, impatience with difficulties, and a feeling of being overwhelmed by the amount of work required. Once again, Mike Mason writes helpfully about this area of discomfort:

> To put it simply, marriage is a relationship far more engrossing than we want it to be. It always turns out to be more than we bargained for. It is disturbingly intense, disruptively involving, and that is exactly the way it was designed to be. It is supposed to be more, almost, than we can handle. It was meant to be a lifelong encounter that would be much more rigorous and demanding than anything human beings ever could have chosen, dreamed of, desired, or invented on their own. After all, we do not even choose to undergo such far-reaching encounters with our closest and dearest friends. Only marriage urges us into these deep and unknown waters. For that is its very purpose: to get us out beyond our depth, out of the shallows of our own secure egocentricity and into the dangerous and unpredictable depths of a real interpersonal encounter.[7]

In Proverbs we read, "Iron sharpens iron, so one man sharpens another" (27:17). This is not a description of one smooth object gently sliding across another, but a process of one rough edge grating against another. The pressure of persons in close contact is the sharpening process by which we are made keen for use—by which our innermost persons are refined and made beautiful.

Conflict, then, does not mean you are a failure. When you own and operate a car, changing the oil every 3000 miles will make your car last for a long time. On many models, if the oil is not changed after a certain period of time, a light will appear on the dashboard: we call this an idiot light. When the light goes on, it doesn't mean that the car's owner is an idiot, merely that he or she is on the threshold of becoming one. Ignore the light, and in time you will become an idiot. Similarly, conflict in marriage simply identifies areas that require maintenance. Conflict doesn't mean you are an idiot—but ignore the conflict, or refuse to attend to the work it asks of you, and in time you will become one.

Good marriages, you see, are never problem-free marriages; instead, a good marriage is one where the partners watch for the warning signals and grow by attending to them. A good marriage is not one where each partner has it all together, perfectly sorted, but one where they are secure enough in God's love for them, and their growing love for one another, that they are not afraid to admit the limits of their capacities. Good marriages create space to be novices, to be awkward, to admit that none of us has very much life skill, that no one is ever ready for marriage, or children, or grows up without regrets. When a couple can operate through their conflicts from the perspective of that kind of security, then the result is always a high and steady growth curve.

We see this again in the words of Robert Browning's poem "Rabbi ben Ezra," the opening line of which romantically invites the listener to "Grow old along with me! / The best is yet to be." Lines 31–32 have the following phrase, "Then welcome each rebuff / that turns earth's smoothness rough." It is easy to make judgments of simplicity; things often appear smooth. But further insight and greater perception, often challenge our initial perceptions. A cue ball to the eye and hand is perfectly smooth. Under a microscope, however, it appears pitted and mountainous. The couple that would take advantage of the opportunity offered by conflict in marriage will permit the new information brought by their spouse to alter their initial perception. Things that on one view appeared smooth on further view become textured. Additionally, a field before being tilled is hard and smooth, but the rebuff of the spade turns its smoothness rough, preparing the soil for fresh fruitfulness. In the same way, the idiot lights of conflict, viewed properly, become opportunities for a harvest of good.

The good news, of course, is that you are never expected to resolve all of these difficulties on your own. When the idiot light signals in your marriage, seek help as soon as the need arises. Wiser people than you have covered this ground before you; call them to your aid. Consult books. Visit counselors, church groups, pastors, seminars, and conferences. Each of these is a resource—like tools and equipment in your gardening shed—that are available to help you grow, as well as heal, your marriage. Do this quickly because unchecked difficulties will compound over time. To humbly seek help is in itself a process that develops life skill, and the best thing the unskilled can do is to surround themselves with wise counselors until they themselves have grown and matured in wisdom.[8] The practice of regularly investing time and energy into this work is precisely the necessary work of your marriage.

Above all other books, invest mutually in the Word of God, the Bible. It is the best guidebook for relationships, for humility, and for growth in the knowledge of self. It has at its heart a model for relationships which is unmatched in any other literature. So read it regularly, and acquire guidance from those who know it. Discuss it, pursue it, and memorize it. Let it lead you into the love of Jesus. And if you continue in that love, in the words of C. S. Lewis, "nothing much can go wrong with you."[9]

FOUR CROSSES

A well-tended house, a raked lawn, and an elderly couple—none of these just happen. And in the same way that there are tools for gardening there are tools for marriage. In addition to humility and the wisdom of counselors, in Christian marriage we have special recourse to the power of God in Christ. In this, we can apply to the help of the cross in four different ways to fend off weeds and increase fruitfulness. The cross, in expressing the high courtesy of heaven toward us, provides the pattern for our own expressions of courtesy to one another.

First, there is the **cross of commitment**. The Scriptures say that "while we were yet sinners, Christ died for us" (Rom. 5:8b). God, it says, made a choice for us when we weren't worthy; He committed to us. This in marriage is the daily choice of commitment that you must make *for* your spouse. You must make it—eagerly and regularly. Take seriously those words of Genesis 2 that the two are becoming "one flesh." Begin to think of yourselves as a unit. When someone asks one partner to do something, ask your spouse—not for *permission*, but because each of you realizes that your choices affect the other person. In all this, the new litmus test for your friends and acquaintances is whether or not they *support* or *denigrate* your marriage. Do not keep company with people who threaten the unity of your marriage.

Second, there is the **cross of accommodation**. We learn in the Scriptures that Christ came down from heaven and became man; He descended to us—He accommodated us—so that we could come to know Him (John 6:38, among others). In the same way you must accommodate one another. Be patient with each other's weaknesses. Allow one another the space to learn and grow together. Give permission to each other to be awkward. Accommodation after this pattern will increase your capacity for happiness and fulfillment in marriage. Again, in selfishness we innately strive to put ourselves first; in accommodation, we strive to put another first, and this is at the heart of the Bible's view of relationships. Accommodation is marked by a desire and willingness on the part of each partner to see and pursue the best for the other, *even in the teeth of all his or her flaws*. This is an investment that keeps the lights of love shining in the eyes of one another.

Third, there is the **cross of self-sacrifice**. When Jesus went to the cross for all mankind, his death not only provided for the forgiveness of sins, it also manifested the high courtesy of Heaven that says, "I offer my life for you." He was willing to give up his life in order for others to have a relationship with God. Christ gave up his life on a cross so that we could live; He gave everything and became the pattern for all our relationships in the process. You will soon learn that the greatest threat to your marriage is selfishness; the lurking desire to do your own thing, and go your own way. So, each day, consider the needs of your partner. Be attentive to his or her needs, and strive actively to meet them. Jesus said to his disciples, "Greater love has no man than this: that he lay down his life for his friends" (John 15:13). Therefore I encourage you to remember the example of Christ, who laid down his life for us, selflessly, so that we could receive the benefits of His Heavenly Father. Show a measure of that great love to each other in bearing the cross of self-sacrifice, and your marriage will thrive for the rest of your lives.

Fourth, and finally, there is the **cross of forgiveness**. Marriage is simply impossible without forgiveness. In the crash of elbows spouses will inevitably wound one another, and progress will demand the will to make things right. The old proverb rings true, that "marriage is the only war in which you sleep with the enemy." You cannot sleep in the same bed with a person for long without practicing forgiveness.

And yet forgiveness is both hard and costly, and costly *because* it is hard. In the act of forgiveness one partner—the wounded, aggrieved partner—willingly cancels his or her suit for damages, personally absorbing the cost of the damages incurred. Forgiving means that the person who wounded me *doesn't* get what he or she deserves. Forgiving means that I personally eat the cost of the other person's wrong—I willingly feel the pain and discomfort of another person's indiscretion. Forgiveness flies in the face of all our concepts of what we, and of what others, deserve.[10]

The strength for all forgiveness is derived from Christ, who forgave us first. In Matthew 18 Jesus tells the story of a king who wished to settle accounts with his servants—to make things just. One servant owed an astronomical amount of money, more than could ever be reasonably repaid in his lifetime. The servant begged for mercy, and the king granted it. But after leaving the king's presence, the servant encountered a fellow servant who owed him a small amount of money. That man also asked for mercy, but the servant who had been forgiven a great deal began to choke him, demanding that the man repay him the small amount, and in the end had the man thrown in jail. The king heard about this and summoned the servant to stand in front of him again, declaring to him, "You wicked slave, I forgave you all that debt because you pleaded with me. Should you not also have had mercy on your fellow slave, in the same way that I had mercy on you?" (Matt. 18:32–33). Then the king ordered this unforgiving servant to be thrown into prison. The meaning of the story is explicit: When God has forgiven us so much—when God Himself in Christ has paid personally the cost of our wrongs—how can we dare to be petty with one another? When we fail to forgive, it is always a failure to draw upon God's forgiveness toward us.

And yet there are other reasons to forgive, because unforgiveness is relationally crippling. In the words of David Augsburger, unforgiveness is cancerous to our relationships because "Hidden hatred turns trust into suspicion, compassion into caustic criticism, and faith in others in to cold cynicism."[11] Forgiveness has the power to break this cycle, and yet to forgive requires a will to suffer. American poet Edna St. Vincent Millay in her baccalaureate hymn, written for her graduation from Vassar in 1917, put it this way: "Lord, let us suffer that we may grow kind."[12] Such a prayer is necessary, because suffering is no guarantee of kindness. Some suffer and grow hard-hearted, calloused and bitter; others become kind and tender even in the midst of terrible suffering and difficulty. What marks the difference whether a person goes one way or the other is the attitude of forgiveness. The failure to forgive when someone hurts us brings an infection to the rest of our attitudes. Our life becomes lived in reaction to our hurts; in unforgiveness we give our hurts authority to govern our life and thoughts. We forfeit our happiness to the one whom we have made the emotional focus of our anger and our unwillingness to forgive. In turn, these infectious seeds of unforgiveness extend to others, generating unkindness, then fixation, then malice, and finally a kind of interior emotional death. In time our attitude extends to all our relationships.

The will to suffer is the will to be human, the will to trust in Christ in the fullness of his humanity. The world is full of angry, bitter people who have not learned to forgive those who have hurt them. Beginning marriage with a commitment to forgive and to be forgiven can be nearly as powerful and liberating as the Cross from which it is modeled. No matter how deep hurts may be, a person willing to forgive can, over time, discover those graces which keep a marriage fresh and vital. Additionally, forgiveness toward those who have hurt us is a creative tool. It allows us to plant new seed in the fallow ground made barren by old hurts and nurtured bitterness. In marriage there will be ample opportunity for the practice of forgiveness, and those who practice it liberally will keep the lights shining in their eyes for one another. After all, who could refuse love to someone who forgives so freely?

These four crosses are powerful tools for a marriage: the crosses of commitment, of accommodation, of self-sacrifice, and of forgiveness are trellises on which every couple would be wise to grow their marriage.

ASSIGNMENT

Sit down together and discuss marriage for a moment. What, at this point, sounds like the most terrifying aspect of marriage? What, at this point, sounds like the most exciting aspect?

PART 1
Undressing for Intimacy

Chapter 2
Undressing Your Stories

Chapter 3
Undressing the Heart

Chapter 4
Undressing the Mind

Chapter 5
Undressing the Soul

CHAPTER 2

Undressing Your Stories

My heart leaps up when I behold
A rainbow in the sky:
So was it when my life began;
So is it now I am a man;
So be it when I shall grow old,
Or let me die!
The Child is father of the Man;
I could wish my days to be
Bound each to each by natural piety.
—William Wordsworth

MR. AND MRS. SMITH: A LESSON IN HISTORY

The 2005 film *Mr. and Mrs. Smith* opens with Brad Pitt and Angelina Jolie in marriage counseling. The camera, situated from the perspective of the therapist, observes their coldness toward one another. They talk past each other, drop snide remarks, and fail to communicate, and while it appears they have come for therapy for problems in their sexual life, it is apparent that the real problems lie elsewhere. This couple lacks intimacy.

As the film progresses we discover that both Smiths are, in fact, highly skilled assassins—a fact that neither knows until their respective agencies hire them to kill one another. Forced by their work to take a fresh, deeper look, the couple begin to see one another, perhaps for the first time. In a critical scene the two of them do battle in the midst of their stately home, destroying everything in sight—figuratively, we might suppose, destroying all the false images of their former, counterfeit life together. Angry passion giving way to sexual, the couple end up making love rather than killing one another. But it is the scenes that follow which are most illuminating.

In the aftermath of their battle, other teams of assassins begin to move in on the house, and Pitt and Jolie must flee together. From their ordinary neighbors they steal a minivan, and a high-speed chase begins. Bullets fly, and for the first time they operate as a team, each person seeing the other doing what that individual does well. While they fight side-by-side they have a conversation—possibly the first *real* conversation they have ever had as a couple.

> "My parents are dead," says Jolie.
> "What?"
> "They died when I was ten."
> "So who was that kindly fellow giving you away at the wedding?"
> "He was a paid actor."
> "I feel so naïve. I feel so naïve for bringing my real parents to the wedding." After a pause, Pitt experiences a sudden realization: "I said, I said I saw your dad on Fantasy Island."[13]

Old expectations, old stories, are stripped away, and for the first time in their marriage the couple get to know one another. "I've never cooked a day in my life," says Jolie. "I never went to university MIT," says Pitt. The entire conversation takes place within a minivan—the emblematic vehicle of a *family*, and the careful viewer will observe, hanging from the rearview mirror, dangling between them in the midst of this first, real conversation, a cross. True intimacy is grounded in history, in trust, and in the friendship of shared knowledge. And in the process of unraveling our pretenses, a new awareness, relationship, and appreciation of our partner can come to life. As the couple unveils their own histories, a fresh grace is unveiled in their relationship.

INTIMACY IN UNDRESSING

Couples in today's world are all too likely to discover, after the wedding, that each has married a *body* he or she knows well but not a *person* they know well. And the truth that cannot be stressed enough is this: **physical intimacy alone will not be enough to sustain a marriage**. The everyday pressures, ups, and downs encountered in ordinary life experience exceed the binding provided by sexual intercourse. If a marriage is to survive, strengthen, and even thrive in the midst of life's imminent complexities, then what must be thoughtfully attended to are each of the more complex kinds of intimacy—of intimacy in sharing history, building friendship, growing an intellectual life together, and enriching yourselves spiritually; of unpacking how we communicate, and understanding gender, and pressing into our woundedness. What is required is a concentrated effort to build the kind of marriage that will bring full intimacy and lasting joy, commitment, mutual respect, and love for a life together. *You are not marrying a body.* You are marrying a person who God made, loves, and desires the best for in this journey of life. And when intimacy is discovered on many levels the sexual connection becomes stronger and longer lasting than it is likely to be when it is the only thing holding the couple together.

This is why preparing for marriage is like learning to undress. This sounds exciting—and it is!—and yet clothing is merely the easiest kind of undressing that we perform. After all, any two strangers can have sex, but it takes a great deal more to make love. Couples who wish to make love out of their lives will do well to make a study of the undressing of the layers and veils that hide our innermost treasures. We read earlier in Genesis 2 that Adam saw Eve, and Eve beheld Adam, and Adam recited his first poem, and then followed the comment, almost as an aside, that "the man and his wife were both naked and were not ashamed" (Gen. 2:25). It would be shallow to conclude that physical nakedness is all that is implied by the author of Genesis here. The couple stand morally and interpersonally naked as well. Their physical nakedness is merely an outward sign of the innermost truth—neither of them has anything to hide.

This deeper nakedness is the true goal of all marriage—and yet it wars against a lifetime of learned covering. Adam and Eve sin before God, and in sin they corrupt their purity. Immediately they hide, sewing together fig leaves to suppress their shame. Then, when God appears, they hide from God—Adam blames Eve (and God, who gave him Eve); Eve blames the snake (and God, who put the snake there); and in this furthered sin of self-deception Adam and Eve hide behind words as well as fig leaves. In their image and likeness we have all learned to cover ourselves. We cover our shame, yes, but we also cover our desires, our hopes, and our dreams. We cover our places of wounding, but also our places of special tenderness. But in marriage a couple is asked to begin to uncover—to strip layer upon layer away from our habits of self-protecting, to *trust* another person with our innermost heart, our most precious thoughts and treasures, in the quiet hope that we can be accepted and loved for who we really are; to be naked, and unafraid.

This is a high and holy calling, and in perspective it makes it all the more regrettable when couples dabble with the physical aspect of nakedness before committing to the deeper, more lasting, and more difficult nakedness of the soul. As humans we are undoubtedly sexual creatures, but we are also far more than merely sexual beings, and marriage is far more complex than simply a sexual union. Sex before marriage is a cheat to true intimacy; it bears the image of marriage, without the content, deceiving couples into thinking they are intimate when in fact they are not. Pursued, it will in time deepen shame rather than resolve it, and inhibit intimacy where it promised to create it. At its worst, it can dehumanize, reducing our partner to a vehicle for personal pleasure, rather than a partner in common life. And this opens the door for a spirit of contempt in both parties—for the woman, because in prioritizing sexual desire over commitment her future husband generates unspoken questions about his character and ability to restrain himself; for the man, because without commitment a sexual relationship with a woman runs the risk of becoming merely a simple conquest.

Imagine an aspiring pilot in flight school who only learned how to take off, but never to land, to navigate weather, to read the dials in the cockpit, or to troubleshoot problems. Such a pilot, were he unlucky enough to actually fly a plane, would almost certainly create a tragedy. In the same way, many marriages are established upon only one kind of intimacy—the sexual—and ignore the myriad other kinds. If we would honor the sheer complexity of human personality then we must acknowledge depths of intimacy beyond the merely sexual. Couples committed to a happy marriage will perform the necessary work to undress at all of these many levels of human intimacy.

A SOLID FOUNDATION IN STORY— UNDRESSING ONE ANOTHER'S HISTORY

What we suggest next is a project and exercise for couples to perform together—and this is meant to be fun! Procure for each of you a notebook or journal in which you can write down significant things about your beloved. Set aside some time and get away to a nice, quiet, cozy place and there take turns sharing and listening to one another, writing down what you hear. This activity—of investing time to discover your partner's life history—is a project that not only can be sustained throughout your engagement, but sets a foundation for conversation that will carry you throughout your marriage. Make it so that the sharing of your life story with your partner is a priority, especially in the months preceding your marriage. Each of you, after all, has a life that was lived before you met, and learning about that life can be an interesting and ongoing part of your relationship.

There are any number of ways to go about this project together. One possibility would be to organize it according to the periods of your life, going through each era and sharing the most significant events and how they affected you. As you cover this historical ground, makes sure that you are getting to know the person's hurts and sorrows, dreams, disappointments, and defining moments. You can begin small with things like where you were born, why you were born there, how your parents happened to live there at that time, and what extended family was there at the time. If you don't know the answers, call up your beloved's mother or father—they will likely be more than happy to fill in the details. Continue to ask further questions: What were your family dynamics? Who were your best family friends growing up? How did your family change when other people were around? What was your school experience like? Who were teachers that impacted your life? Where did your family go on vacations? What were these vacations like? How were the family interactions? Where were you in the birth order and how did that define you as a person? The questions can be endless, and together you can chase them with the delight of children opening packages on Christmas morning.

In an exercise such as this one, follow-up questions are just as important as the initial information—not only because they reveal the interest of your partner, but because they invite further and deeper reflection into our own histories. Each partner should practice listening attentively, asking questions that get to the deeper matters. "What did that feel like?" "Do you remember that often?" "Was that move hard for you?" "How did your parent's divorce affect you?" Asking questions about our emotions surrounding these memories is a powerful way to re-access the memories themselves, and learning to ask such questions that encourage a person to go deeper will help the relationship grow.

In addition to talking about these experiences, you may even want to visit the historical places relevant to your partner's life if you grew up in different locations. It is always interesting to see where they lived, played as children, went to school, and even meet old friends and relatives. If you can't do all this while engaged, you can plan it in the future years and include it in your notebooks, snapping photos along the way and collecting other memorabilia. Such a project could in time become something special to pass down to your children.

All of these recommendations, of course, are simply guidelines—as a couple you are free to be as creative as you want to be. We have seen couples who have expanded this project much further. The key is to establish an attitude of abiding interest in the wholeness and complexity of the person you plan to marry. As Wordsworth wrote in the poem quoted at the beginning of this chapter, "The child is the father of the man."[14] When we spread the table of our memories before one another we are bearing witness to the child, the adolescent, and young adult who gives shape to your personalities today.

Developing historical intimacy in this way lays a foundation for all the other forms of intimacy, not only because it invites a fully orbed knowledge of your spouse, but because the way that we engage this kind of conversation also shapes how we communicate. There are some very important factors that shape this historical conversation and can with intentionality extend to all your conversations.

The dominant factor is *vulnerability*. The willingness to open up and speak to your partner about the significant events that have shaped your life requires a kind of risk. These are memories that you may never have spoken to another soul in your life. The choice to be vulnerable in that moment is a choice, profoundly, to trust. For many people, it would be much easier to take off their *actual* clothes than the emotional clothes that cover their life stories! But the work must not be avoided, and the man or woman who refuses to be vulnerable also refuses to trust. In such an environment intimacy can never truly grow.

Vulnerability is also powerful as a door to your own self-knowledge. As your partner asks questions about your life, following the trail of the conversation wherever it goes, insights and revelations about your own story can emerge. Vulnerability means not only sharing what has been private, but also permitting someone else to offer perspective on your story. The person who refuses to be vulnerable not only fails to be intimate with someone else, but he also fails to truly know himself.

When these conversations range into vulnerable matters, it is very important that the listening partner honor the vulnerability of the sharer. Imagine what it would feel like to stand naked in front of your partner, and then to have that person point at some part of your body, and laugh, or to ignore you while looking at a phone or television screen. Would you feel valued in that tender moment? If the answer is no, then consider how you can strive to give value to the memories shared with you. This, fundamentally, is an activity of listening and accepting; you are not listening in order to pass judgment. For the sharing partner, it is an opportunity to be accepted for things that you alone know about your life. Ensure that you honor one another in the sharing of these often-precious memories.

These moments of undressing offer an unprecedented opportunity to share our deepest secrets, and secrets we cannot talk about control us. If there are places in your life you cannot reveal to the person you are going to marry, not only are you implicitly saying that it's okay to have secrets in this relationship, but to that same degree you are implying that you do not trust your partner. This might indicate either that your partner is untrustworthy, or in fact that you yourself are untrusting. But if you are willing to take the risk you might discover levels of trust that you never before anticipated.

There are times when individuals have experienced past events that they would rather forget, and they might because of this have a difficult time sharing. A block to sharing like this informs you that there are some deep issues that may need to be addressed.[15] Nevertheless, we must recognize that becoming intimate involves sharing your whole self—the good, the bad, and the ugly. If your partner cannot handle hearing about the past things in your life that were difficult for you, that person may not be the one for you. Jerry once knew a woman who confided in her fiancé that when she was a teenager she had an abortion. Unable to cope with this information, her fiancé broke off the engagement, breaking her heart in the process. Several years later she met another man and again confided in him. This time, when she had shared her story, he took her in his arms and said, "I'm so sorry you had to go through that. I love you even more for sharing such a deep hurt with me." They went on to have four children of their own, and she even became involved in a pro-life organization. Sharing these hurts before marriage establishes a clear foundation for your relationship and can also provide unprecedented and unexpected opportunities for healing.

If you find that you *cannot* share your past with the person you love, you should probably find out why that is the case. Secrets kept early in the relationship typically erupt later, and quite possibly in a destructive manner. We have found that often when couples share these deep parts of themselves, the other person sincerely makes an effort to show acceptance and tell the person they love how much closer they feel. Love multiplies where vulnerability is sincere. And the truth of the matter is that we each have things in our past we are ashamed of, from acts we did or were done to us, to thoughts we had or have. True intimacy develops where couples embrace the risk and take the courage to share their lives with one another.

There is one more thing to be kept in mind. Historical undressing demands that we guard the secrets that are shared with us. Inasmuch as we hear these stories without judgment—accepting that the story is simply part of the person sitting beside us—we must also be good stewards of that which is shared with us. In marriage, your secrets are mine, and my secrets are yours, and together we hold them in trust for one another. And by building such a foundation on the basis of openness, honesty, and acceptance, you establish a great trajectory for your future family.

ASSIGNMENT ·

Purchase some notebooks and set aside some time to undress historically. The following questions are guidelines to help you get started:

Where were you born?

What was your home like?

What were your parents like?

How many siblings did you have?

Who were you closest to in your family?

Who were your family's closest friends?

What are some significant memories from your childhood home?

What's your earliest memory?

Did you have pets growing up?

Who were your best friends when you were a child?

What was a perfect summer day, growing up?

Who was your favorite teacher?

What was your favorite subject?

Did you play sports? Which ones?

Did your family go on vacations together?

What was your favorite home-cooked meal?

What is your saddest memory from childhood?

Have you ever had a close relative pass away?

What was it like when your body changed? (For example, a
first period, or memories of your voice changing, etc.)

Do you remember the first girl/boy who captured your heart?

Were you ever bullied in school?

What's your favorite childhood memory?

Who was your first kiss?

What is your relationship with your parents like, now that
you're an adult?

Who have you dated?

How did those relationships end?

Have you been sexually active in the past?

How many partners have you had?

Where have you been in the world?

When do you feel emotionally high?

What makes you feel emotionally low?

Where do you see deficiencies in your life/character today?

Where would you like to see yourself grow in the future?

Note: Questions about sexual history can be tricky. But we must consider the alternatives. On the one hand, a partner can hide his or her sexual history from the other. But what happens if it is exposed later on when you encounter a former partner, or new information comes to light? Would you not rather know the whole story now, than discover it later at happenstance? Especially for men today, pornography addiction is a real struggle. If you struggle, there is no nobility in deceiving your spouse before your marriage, only for her to discover and be betrayed by it in the course of your marriage. Quite simply total honesty before marriage is the best option for couples who want to go into marriage with their eyes open and their heads on straight.

CHAPTER 3

Undressing the Heart

The world will never starve for want of wonders, but only for want of wonder.
—G. K. Chesterton

WONDER

Couples who would thrive in love would do well to ask themselves the question, often, "What must God be like?" When Jerry first asked this it was when Voyager, the interplanetary probe, went speeding out past Saturn, that most mysterious, ringed planet. After the pictures were sent back he rushed to get his copy of *Time*, and couldn't wait for the *National Geographic*. When they arrived it was only to discover that the outer ring of Saturn is *braided*. They call it the F-ring, and physicists continue to marvel at it. What must God be like, who for His own good pleasure, though no human eye had seen it, chose to braid the outer ring of Saturn? Jerry explained this to a friend, who said, "Yeah, and Jerry, we don't know if He didn't just braid it for the picture."

We think of ships that park themselves over the depths of the ocean greater than the light of the sun can reach. There they dangle cameras on tethers and take pictures of fish painted neon bright. It's not for camouflage; it's not to attract a mate. (As a matter of fact, how *do* fish at those depths get together?) But we might think, What must God be like, who for His own good pleasure, though no human eye had seen it, chose to paint fish in the invisible depths neon bright?

We can think of palm trees silhouetted against an auburn sunset sky, mountain ranges silhouetted against an auburn sunset sky, or, if you're from the Great Plains, even a corn field silhouetted against an auburn sunset sky. That should be enough to provoke awe and wonder. We could have lived on a dark planet and been told there would be a single sunset. People would line the West coast of every continent and every island, and regale their progeny with the wonder of that event. And yet—what must God be like who has made our planet a perpetual kaleidoscope of sunrises and sunsets, and that people would see it and their hearts be flooded with awe and wonder?

One star twinkling in the night sky should have been enough, but God has been so liberal with His glory that we get stars, and moons, and galaxies, and comets, and northern lights. G. K. Chesterton once said that "one elephant having a trunk was odd, but all elephants having trunks looked like a plot."[16] God has plots and purposes and designs— what must He be like?

In the midst of all those wonders there was a little boy and a little girl who were each knit together in the womb of their mothers by the sovereign hand of God, each a person crafted with magnificent care and purpose. They were born, grew, fell in love, and now marry—each no less marvelous than the braided ring of Saturn, or rainbowed fish at the depths of the sea, or the stars in the heavens; each a testimony to the sovereign grace of a God who for His own good pleasure has chosen to bring you two together. What must God be like?

G. K. Chesterton wrote, "The world will never starve for want of wonders, but only for want of wonder."[17] "Want" here means lack, or absence—in other words, the world will never have a shortage of wonders—things at which we *ought* to marvel—but it will often have a shortage of wonder itself, of people attending to and marveling at the magnificence, the bounty, and the glory of God's creative hand. Couples who are in love have an eye turned toward one another. The groom looks at his bride, into her life, her past, her heart, and she looks into his, and if they have the right attitude, they will never starve for want of wonder, because in one another they will perceive the unveiling of each other's innermost heart as a wondrous treasure generated by God.

AN INVITATION TO EXPERTISE

Paul in 1 Corinthians 8:1 says that "knowledge puffs up, while love builds up" (NIV). As you learn your spouse—her interests, passions, history, and life story—you are increasing your knowledge not for the sake of knowledge, but expressly for the sake of love. This is an invitation to *really know* this other person in a way you know nobody else in your life. He who knows his wife well is capable of loving her well. In this way your ever-increasing knowledge of your spouse is an invitation to a kind of expertise. You are being invited, as a husband or wife, to become the world's leading expert at loving that person. You are aspiring to be the only, unique, earthly lover of his or her life.

This is a lifelong task. A friend of Jeremy's once remarked to a classroom full of students that "the day you've figured out your spouse is the day your marriage ends." This statement left many students mystified, but if you think about it there's real truth in it. The day you stop learning about your spouse, the day you stop believing that he or she is a person worth studying, worth learning about, worth going deeper with, is the day your sense of wonder dies, and therefore the day your marriage dies. You have moved from an attitude of wonder to one of contempt. If you truly know everything about him, then he is beneath your interest, and in some sense under your control. A heart of wonder is a certain tonic against such a trap.

As you learn your spouse's history, preferences, and needs, you will want to make special account of the differences that gender play in this process. We'll speak more about gender in a few chapters, but for now I want to suggest that loving effectively will mean acknowledging the role that gender plays in shaping what we expect from a partner. Women, wired to nurture, often have a high need for security. This manifests itself in relationships in a desire to be cherished—to know that your spouse's love is secure. Consider—when you (a woman) are preparing for a date and have groomed yourself, chosen your outfit, fixed your hair, and selected jewelry and a handbag, the moment you first present yourself to your partner is actually quite a tender moment. The unwise man will miss the opportunity to speak his love in such a moment—whether by ignoring it, or by criticizing her appearance. (And be honest—if he criticizes your appearance in that moment, it does not bode well for the evening.) The wise man will ensure that he has prepared a compliment to honor her preparation and speak into her heart. Liesel likes to be romanced, and romance for Liesel means *planning*. Knowing that Jeremy has prepared in advance for her gives her a sense that she is loved. Jeremy, however, happens to be a superb on-the-fly kind of guy. It isn't his first nature to make plans like that! But knowing this about his wife gives him the knowledge he needs to love her more effectively.

For men, the deepest need may be for partnership. This goes back to the Garden of Eden and the creation of Eve, whose design and purpose was to be, not a servant of Adam, but a helper in his life's work. The woman who wants to show love to her husband will do well to find ways to partner with and support his life's work. Jeremy, as a pastor and writer, wishes for partnership and understanding in both those tasks, and feels well-loved when Liesel comes alongside those tasks to support and encourage him. Most men feel profoundly diminished when their spouses criticize their life dreams—especially when they ridicule them in public.[18]

Naturally, dividing gender in this way doesn't mean that men don't desire to be cherished, nor that women do not wish for partnership, but in general our biology leads us into a propensity toward these responses. Regardless, it is only when you truly *know* the other person that you will be capable of loving them at this deep, inward level.

Acknowledging that we each receive love in different ways is actually a very important step in growing together as a couple. Gary Chapman's well-known book *The Five Love Languages* is very helpful here. In the book Chapman outlines five different ways that people like to *receive* love. Words of Affirmation mean that I feel loved when my spouse says nice things to me. Quality Time means that I feel loved when my spouse spends dedicated time with me. Receiving Gifts means that I feel loved when my spouse presents me with a gift. Acts of Service means I feel loved when my spouse does things for me (chores, or tasks, etc.). Physical Touch means I feel loved when my spouse reaches out to touch me, whether holding a hand or hugging. The key, when we examine these "love languages" is to acknowledge that *how I like to receive love may be different from how my spouse likes to receive love.* I may resonate strongly with Quality Time, but my wife might prefer Acts of Service. This only becomes a problem because we typically attempt to communicate love in the language with which we are most familiar—in other words, I will attempt to offer Quality Time to my wife when what she really wants is for me to take out the trash, or she will make me a lunch when what I really want is to sit down with her and watch a movie. Once again, it is our increasing knowledge of the other person which equips us to love him or her in the best possible way.[19]

Ultimately, as you undress these things together keep in mind that these exercises are never about snooping or investigative journalism, but the cultivation of a deep fascination for one another. Another way we might describe this is to say that the bride and groom, through their focused attention on one another, are building a kind of "Love Map."[20] A Love Map describes the space in your brain which you reserve for your partner—things, facts, and details that you keep in store. If you are technologically savvy, then your love map is the specially partitioned hard drive space in your mind, set apart for your spouse alone. In this, it is a real measure of the regard you bear for your partner.

Imagine for a moment a groom who has at his mental fingertips all the Yankee baseball statistics for the past 100 years. He can tell you who played second base in 1934, as well as the number of hits, runs, and errors of that player. Imagine the groom having all that knowledge, but not knowing his bride's dress size. Wouldn't you think something was out of proportion? Imagine a bride who has memorized the entire cast roster of a favorite show—knowing all their details, aspirations, motives, and dialogue—but doesn't know her groom's interests and aspirations. Wouldn't you think something was off? John Gottman tells the story of a man who was so busy with his work that he didn't know the name of his family dog. In each case something is amiss with regard to regard, and our attentiveness to our partner's life is a direct measure of our investment into the other person. The space you invest in learning his or her life is *important.*

FROM INTEREST TO LOVE

As you learn about this magnificent, worthy-of-wonder other person it is terribly important that you continue to learn about yourself as well. Relationships usually begin with interest in another person. Your gaze is fixed on *her*, and hers on *him*, and as you look at one another that interest grows into passion and eventually what we call love. Yet here we must interject a warning—if only simply to remember that *all passions are temporary*.

In all likelihood you can recognize this from your own experience. When I (Jeremy) was a kid I used to long for new Lego sets. Christmas only really felt like Christmas when I had something to build in the afternoon after we'd opened presents in the morning. When you were a child and Christmas was approaching, did you ever experience that special longing for a certain toy? Whether a game, or a doll, or a gadget? In our hearts, it was easy to come to imagine that the toy would fulfill all our longings, and in our acute desire we came to believe the toy was the answer to our deepest needs. But here's the catch—how many of us are *still* playing with that toy, gadget, or doll? Aren't all these gifts either discarded or gathering dust somewhere? We understand, implicitly, that all of our passions fade.

Many modern people are under the assumption that somehow, contrary to all the evidence we possess otherwise, the passion of marriage can continue unabated—that a truly thriving marriage is one where the couple, in love, cascades into greater and greater experiences of being "in love." But this attitude is dangerous for a number of crucial reasons. C. S. Lewis voices the first danger for us this way (note—the word "maundering" means "talking dreamily"):

> But if you decide to make thrills your regular diet and try to prolong them artificially, they will all get weaker and weaker, and fewer and fewer, and you will be a bored, disillusioned old man for the rest of your life. It is because so few people understand this that you find many middle-aged men and women maundering about their lost youth, at the very age when new

horizons ought to be appearing and new doors opening all round them."[21]

The person, in other words, who turns to thrills—to the experience of passion—to give meaning and significance to life is setting himself or herself up for certain disappointment. This is, in part, because the impact of thrills diminishes over time, like the person who has become so accustomed to salting his food that his tongue is seared and he is no longer capable of tasting other flavors. In the same way, a fixation on passion will in time rob an individual of the capacity to appreciate the more normal, ordinary pleasures of life.

But this leads to the second danger—that of failing to appreciate the value of commitment. Passions have their own wonderful purpose—they grab our attention and give us impetus to move forward. But passion, if it is to bear genuine fruit, must be joined together with commitment. There is all the difference in the world between saying that "I love to play the guitar!" and actually *knowing* how to play. In fact, between the initial passion of picking up a new instrument and the level of expertise required to be proficient and truly enjoy playing the instrument lies nearly countless hours of practice, failure, and difficulty. The difference between the passionate and the proficient player is measured, then, by commitment.

A couple standing at the altar to wed one another is reaching the end of "love" as they have known it and the beginning of "love" as it is in marriage. In this, married love is a very different thing from the love when you fell "in love"—it is deeper, and more difficult, but also far more rewarding. It is not the one-time vow that will carry us through in marriage, but the daily, sometimes hourly, *choice* which we make for our spouse that is the bread and butter of a marriage.

All the same, being "in love" is a lot of fun. During the time that we are in love we feel like and act like the person we always want to be. We are our best selves; we love, we are magnanimous, we are creative, and we are forgiving. That experience of being in love is the greatest promise that an individual human receives—it foreshadows the kind of person we wish we could be all the time; it strikes at our selfishness and sinfulness.

But, after a time, the promise has to become a reality. The dream of becoming a better person must move beyond being merely a dream. After all, we don't just want to live in a wonderful but unfulfilled state of life. Imagine if you went to IKEA and purchased a truckload of new furniture for your home. You walked through those little rooms and thought, "Ooo, I'd like this! And this! And *this!*" Imagine going through all the hard work of choosing, purchasing, and transporting your dream furniture, but then leaving it unassembled in boxes around your home. Is it enough to leave the furniture in that state, never built, gathering dust? When guests come over would you ask them to sit in your unassembled chairs, to eat at your unassembled table? You understand with IKEA that to make the vision a reality you must pass through the hard work of assembling your furniture, the difficult process of wrestling with heavy boxes, obscure instructions, and little wrenches, all so that you can enjoy your home. The same thing is true for marriage, because at some point for each of us the hard work must begin. That's when the fire of love seems to die, and the more mature love must arise to take its place. This is also where many people quit; they give up on marriage because they have lost sight of the vision. They have confused the first kind of love with the more mature second kind. And the difficult truth is this: while being in love gives us a *vision* of who we really want to be— like shopping in IKEA—really loving is the hard work of becoming that person in community.

Love, therefore, is hard work. It *costs* us to love. While we're in love the cost seems cheap—the cost of magnanimity, of forgiveness, of commitment, of self-sacrifice, the cost of being our best selves, the cost of putting aside our pettiness, our grievances, our frustrations—all of these costs we give up freely. That's part of the fun! And so, when we are in love, we spend freely; but when we get married it is time to begin paying the cost to be the people we want to be. That means we are faced with a decision: we must apply our will to accomplish the vision we have received. We must choose to commit.

That is why we make a promise to one another before God, our friends, and our families, to continue the path toward becoming the person you dream you can be—the person you so easily are when in love. The promise of marriage is the promise to stick to one other when the in-love part of your relationship passes away. It is a promise to continue to learn to be fully human in the company of another person—one who is making the very same commitment to you.

This cannot be stressed enough—marriage *is* the promise. It is the covenant commitment made between two people to tough it out together *no matter what* until one of them dies. It is the recognition that our passions and feelings are temporary—that we will have bad days, bad weeks, or even bad years, but that our commitment to one another supersedes any and all concerns—that's the meaning of those words in the traditional vow, "in sickness and in health, for richer or for poorer, until we are parted by death." Actress Jamie Lee Curtis was once asked how it was that her marriage to Christopher Guest had survived 31 years. Her answer was simple: "Don't get divorced." She went on to say, "I could write a book on marriage called 'Don't Leave.'"[22] Her advice is profound only because it has been so often forgotten.

For the Christian, especially, divorce is never really an option. Making it an option begins the work of poisoning your thoughts about your own commitment to marriage. People rarely use paper dictionaries any longer, but if you still own one open up to the entry for divorce alongside your spouse. Read the definition through together, then take a permanent marker and cross the word out from the dictionary as a testimony to yourselves, and to one another, that divorce won't be an option for you. The challenge is simply to eliminate the concept from your mind, and replace it with an attitude of "no matter what." Ruth Graham, wife of Billy Graham, once said, "I've never considered divorce." She went on to remark, wryly, "Murder, yes, but not divorce."[23] The strength of the promise we make to one another in marriage is such that, in a very real way, murder is more acceptable than breaking the promise (not that we advocate murdering your spouse!).

Commitment, then, gives direction to our passion, provides stability amidst our shifting passions, and offers security and comfort in the sharing of history and life together.

ASSIGNMENT

Set aside some time to discuss your expectations and experiences with regard to love and commitment. The following questions can help get you started:

How do you like to receive love?

How does your partner like to receive love?

How did your family express love when you were growing up?

What do you think it means to commit to one another, no matter what?

Consider the traditional wedding vows for a moment and examine each part—what is it you are promising to do for one another?

I, _____, take you _____ to be my lawfully wedded wife/ husband, to have and to hold from this day forward, for better or for worse, for richer or for poorer, in sickness and in health, until we are parted by death. This is my solemn vow.

CHAPTER 4

Undressing the Mind

Lovers are always talking to one another about their love; Friends hardly ever talk about their Friendship. Lovers are normally face to face, absorbed in each other; Friends, side by side, absorbed in some common interest.
—C. S. Lewis

LOOKING AT, LOOKING ALONGSIDE

*E*very wedding seems to focus on the moment when a bride comes down the aisle. Ushers close the doors, the attendees stand, the flower girl has littered the aisle with petals, and then the bride enters the room, radiant, on the arm of her father. Personally, I (Jeremy) always like to look at the groom at this moment and see his expression. Very often, while all eyes are on the bride, a strange mist appears to form in his eyes and he has to fight back tears. It is a precious moment. Then, once the bride and groom are side by side and I begin speaking the words of invocation and the charge to the couple, it becomes clear that neither one is listening to me in particular—they are too focused on one another, too focused on the emotions of the moment—anticipation, joy, wonder, trepidation, and a whole host of other feelings simply cascading through their hearts. It is one of the tenderest moments in their young lives.

To look *at* one another is precisely what lovers do. Their gaze is affixed upon one another, and their sense of the beauty and wonder of the other person eclipses other elements from their sight. Thus far, as we've talked about undressing history and the heart, we've had in view this first kind of looking—the looking at. The gaze is focused on the beloved, to see and perceive all that is within the heart and all that is contained in your beloved's story so that you can love that person effectively. Throughout this process you have been challenged to undergo all such looking with Chesterton's maxim that "The world will never starve for want of wonders, but only for want of wonder." And yet there is another kind of looking—the looking that happens alongside. What we're talking about now is learning to undress intellectually.

Intellectual undressing catalyzes many areas of growth as a couple. It begins with developing an interest in those interests and hobbies your partner brings to the marriage. You come to see what they see and love what they love, and this in turn gives you fresh insight into the kind of person they are. While together you grow as a couple, you also grow as a person under the influence of your partner's passions and experiences that expand your horizons. A spirit of curiosity, and an openness to new experiences, builds a platform that can enrich your marriage for years to come. It inaugurates adventures, and new interests into your common life together. In time, you yourself become more interesting. It adds knowledge to familiar areas and can make you think of people that others like to be around. It becomes the basis for your own family's interests, rituals, and experiences.

Maybe a series of Venn Diagrams can help to illustrate what we mean by this more clearly. Consider the first:

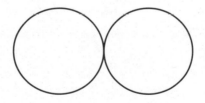

When a couple meet, their interests intersect on the mere boundary. She looks beautiful, he appears to be interesting, we both have this location, or these other people, in common. The relationship begins on the boundary and proceeds from there. In time, it begins to look more like this:

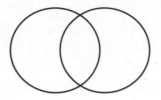

Here the couple have quite a few more shared interests, as well as shared history. They've been on dates, and created memories, and they find there are a number of things they have in common—similar music, similar books, similar activities. As they mature in intimacy the relationship eventually comes to look like this:

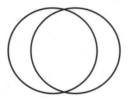

Note, clearly, that mature intimacy is not *sameness*. A couple never reaches the place where 100% of each partner's interests are identical to the other partner's. Each of you will maintain hobbies, interests, and even friends that are not shared. Nevertheless, couples who have committed to a process of intellectual undressing will cultivate a significant overlap of interests together.

Some of the most fascinating couples we have met are those that have addressed this area in their marriage. We love to be around them. They make us curious to learn new things. They bring others into their adventures. Their children get involved. Their friends get involved. They have so much to talk about that they long to be together, even after years of being married. Life is never boring because they are never bored. There is always something new to learn and share with their mate. The ideas are endless! What fun you will have as you explore and learn about each other's passions, hobbies, interests, talents, and loves!

Let us give you some personal examples. When we (Jerry and Claudia) were married, we each came with our individual interests. One was interested in music, the arts, and other cultures. The other was an excellent athlete who loved football. We both loved literature, English history, traveling, and antiques.

During high school Claudia's family had hosted a foreign exchange student from Italy for a year. Later, during college, she had the opportunity to visit her Italian sister's family in Italy and travel throughout Europe for a summer. She spent time in Holland seeing her grandparents' native country and visiting with family friends. Jerry had never had the opportunity to travel overseas. He had worked in the mountains at YMCA camps during his summers, had played football during college, and started reading the books of C. S. Lewis. When we got married we purposed to explore the interests of the other. We created dates that included attending concerts and sports events. We went on vacations where we explored common interests. We spent intentional time getting involved in what the other enjoyed and to learn about it.

After hearing about Claudia's adventures in Europe Jerry wanted to travel. Since we both had a love for and interest in England and its literature, the summer after we were married we decided to visit England and Scotland. Jerry's family roots were Scottish and we wanted to see the places his ancestors had lived. We also wanted to see places mentioned in the books we had read. We didn't have a lot of money but we had a lot of energy! Our first project was to buy Winston Churchill's *History of the English-Speaking Peoples*, all four volumes of it. It sounds overwhelming, but these books are actually quite short, well-written, and full of fascinating history. We read them aloud on quiet evenings during the months before we left. We bought travel books, maps, cheap airline tickets, and train passes for three weeks. We marked individual places of interest on the map and connected the dots. That became our itinerary. Claudia wanted to see Canterbury, English gardens, and the museums of London. Jerry was mostly interested in Oxford and the world of C. S. Lewis. We added other places from our reading of Churchill such as Stonehenge, various cathedrals, and the Lake District. Before long we had planned a circular trip around Great Britain.

One of the most exciting adventures of that trip was traveling up to Scotland. We wanted to see Jerry's family's castle, named Grant Castle, Grantown-On-Spey, and the Spey Valley (where the finest whiskey in the world is made). We had read in Churchill's history books about a tiny, one-mile-long island off the northern coast of Scotland named Iona. Remote, it is a sacred place to the Scots since it is where Christianity was first brought to Scotland by St. Columba, the patron saint of Scotland. It is also where over 30 Scottish Kings are buried. Traveling by train through the heather-covered mountains, by bus along the Loch Ness on one-lane roads filled with local people, and by small motor boat to get to Iona was one of the most interesting things we did on our trip. We reached our destination on a rainy afternoon after crossing from the city of Oban, across the Island of Mull where Robert Louis Stevenson set his famous classic *Kidnapped*, and finally to the little island of Iona. What memories we have of that little side trip!

We learned to be creative because we did not have a lot of money to spend. Most days we bought sandwiches and other food at a local market and stayed in B&B's, much more fun than eating in fancy restaurants and staying in hotels. This trip proved to be a catalyst for the projection of our life in many ways. Jerry has since gone on to make C. S. Lewis one of his life's interests. Claudia found an interest in church history, the Queen of England's favorite dog, a Welsh Corgi, and cottage gardening. Later in our life we were able to take all four of our children to Oxford and live in England for six months while Jerry studied the writings of C. S. Lewis. It was only the beginning of many other adventures that have come out of that trip we took together in our early years of marriage.

Another additional aspect of intellectual intimacy that you can do together is choosing new activities or interests that you both can grow in. These may come from discussions you have about things you have seen or read. They may come from hearing others' ideas. You may find other couples who have similar interests and do things together. Keep yourselves curious. Challenge each other to grow in new areas.

Encourage one another in new vistas. Listen to each other. Include each other. Be excited for each other.

FRIENDSHIP AND DATING

As we hope you can see, these shared interests become the basis of your ongoing friendship as a couple. And it is important to note that a couple with good experiences together, common interests, and positive regard is significantly buffered against the everyday stresses of life in the world and life together. A couple who commit to being and becoming friends very nearly guarantees the success of their marriage as well as a high level of relational happiness.

Why should this be the case? Consider something C. S. Lewis wrote in his book on the four loves,

> Lovers are always talking to one another about their love; Friends hardly ever talk about their Friendship. Lovers are normally face to face, absorbed in each other; Friends, side by side, absorbed in some common interest.[24]

The gaze *at*, while wonderful, is insufficient to keep a couple throughout life—there must also be a gaze *alongside*. In this, the couple strive to find places of commonality—shared books, shared experiences, shared interests—that will keep them fresh and interesting as the years progress. All too often it happens that couples neglect this critical aspect of their relationship, allowing work, then children, to crowd out their investment in one another. The result, tragically, is that at some point the children move out of the home and the husband and wife discover to their mutual dismay that they are married to a virtual stranger. If you would have love thrive in your marriage for the long term, you would be wise to seek to share passions beyond simply one another.

Many couples implicitly feel that dating belongs to the time before marriage, and that once they are married they no longer need to date. Indeed, many challenges begin to arise as life becomes more complex. Finances, children, hiring babysitters—these things can make dating your spouse seem like more trouble than it's worth. But dating clearly is a key way to continue to develop friendship and interest with one another—whether it be eating at a favorite restaurant, or seeing the latest film together, going on a walk, attending a play, sitting on a blanket together in a park, or simply getting dessert and talking. A date is an activity that bridges the gap between the gaze that looks at your spouse, and the gaze that looks together with your spouse. In the words of the author of Ecclesiastes,

> Two are better than one because they have a good return for their labor. For if either of them falls, the one will lift up his companion. But woe to the one who falls when there is not another to lift him up. Furthermore, if two lie down together they keep warm, but how can one be warm alone? And if one can overpower him who is alone, two can resist him. A cord of three strands is not quickly torn apart. (Ecclesiastes 4:9–12)

Perhaps, in this circumstance, the third strand of the cord that strengthens a couple is their cultivated interest in subjects that bring life to their relationship—in their commitment to friendship, dating, and a life together grounded in a look alongside one another.

CREATING A NEW FAMILY

Such interests also become the basis not only for your friendship with other couples, but also for your experiences with your children. Genesis 2:24 again says, "For this reason a man will leave his father and his mother and be joined to his wife; and they shall become one flesh." The two people who leave behind the home of their parents nevertheless bring interests and passions with them—but together, God willing, they will also create a new human—one who is in every way a representation of the "one flesh" of their marriage. In this very astonishing way, your children will be the direct recipients of your shared intellectual life. In other words, a cultivated intellectual life benefits your children as well, because it ought to be developed inclusively with them. In fact, there will be many years where they and their activities will be the focus of your interests and attention. Get involved in what they enjoy and permit them to bring the world to you in a fresh way. One of the best ways to stay young is to remain open to the new experiences that children bring into our homes. Make a habit of attending their activities as a couple. Get involved serving as volunteers together in their schools and events. But do not neglect exposing them to some of your interests as well. They will be richer people for it, and they will learn from your example what it means to have a wonderful, exciting marriage and family life.

We once heard about a couple with young children who went to Hawaii for a vacation. They had a glorious time and while there got a great idea. The parents decided to find a remote place on the island and bury a letter and a special gift there for their children. They planned what it would be, bought it, buried it, and made a special "treasure map" of the hidden spot where it was buried. Years later, on one of their special anniversaries, they took their whole family to Hawaii and gave the "treasure map" to their children. What an adventure they all had as the children followed the map and found the treasure!

Many of these intellectual interests can also be quite ordinary, and it is a good idea for couples to take time to discuss the various rituals that they think should have presence in their lives. For example, what are the foods you like to eat when you're feeling sick? How do you like to celebrate birthdays? What happens when mom or dad comes home from work? How often do we eat together as a family? Will we celebrate Christmas on Christmas Eve or Christmas Day? How do you like to celebrate birthdays? Each topic offers an opportunity for you as a couple to explore and choose how you will pass these things on to your children. For example, Liesel's family always purchased a cookie cake for birthdays. This was unheard of to Jeremy, but Jeremy liked cookies and knew how to bake, so he figured out how to make a cookie cake at home. Now that we've got three kids, we get to eat a lot of cookie cake each year, but we feel that birthdays aren't the same without them! A marriage in time becomes peppered with countless such myths, rituals, and hobbies—each unique to the couple.[25]

THE LIFE OF THE MIND

In addition to opening yourselves to the interests and passions of your spouse, a good habit to develop that will assist toward a successful marriage is to read a good book on marriage each year. In the same way that it takes a mechanic to know how to take care of the problems in a car, we require an outside perspective to know how to keep marriages strong. Reading a book per year helps couples to keep their thinking sharp about the many complex areas that arise within the entwining of two lives. As the years pass, you will in time collect a library of good books on marriage, a visible testimony to your commitment to maintaining the upkeep of your marriage.

As a rule, we think each partner should choose a different book each year. The primary reason is that reading your own book forces you to read for yourself, and it prevents you in part from reading it for your spouse. There is a great temptation, when looking into marriage, to jump to criticism of our partner and overlook the work that has to be done in our own hearts. Reading a book on your own is a good way to keep you honest and focused on your own work in this process.

That doesn't mean couples can't invest in material to work on their marriage together; quite the opposite, it is beneficial to listen to talks, or attend seminars, weekends away, and camps. We (all four of us) often read to each other on long drives. One person reads a chapter while the other drives. We stop after each chapter or at a significant point and process how we think and feel about it. This is a great time to share ideas, thoughts, and feelings.

It is a good idea to diversify the kinds of materials you are encountering, making sure that you cover a variety of topics such as communication, finance, sex, raising children, living with in-laws, or the many other subjects that will come up in your life together. When children come, you might add a parenting book per year to your reading as well. Starting this habit early in marriage will create an atmosphere of openness to learn and communicate vulnerability and willingness to change as new challenges reveal themselves.

Naturally, you will also want to make the Bible a regular part of your common reading as well. Simply put, the Bible is the best guide-book for relationships. It has at its core the best relationship model available, and it provides access to the mind that crafted the universe. Therefore you will do well to read it regularly and seek guidance from those who know it. Discuss it, pursue it, memorize it, and make it a part of the fabric of your married life.

In all this, undressing intellectually is only the beginning of many years of adventures together. Plan now some areas you would like to cultivate. Choose something personal from each of you and then choose something together that you would like to pursue. Encouraging your partner's gifts, interests, and talents shows love in a unique way that other areas do not address. Truly, if you intentionally bring this aspect into your relationship, you will never "want of wonders."

ASSIGNMENT

Undressing Intellectually incorporates how you dream about your future. Consider the following questions as starting points to dream about your future together:

When you look ten years down the line, what are some things you'd like to accomplish?

When you look fifty years down the line, what are some things you'd like to have accomplished?

What are some dreams and aspirations you bring to your marriage?

If you were given an airline ticket to anywhere in the world, where would you go?

If you could live in any city in the world, where would you live?

If you could learn a musical instrument, what would you learn?

If you had time for any hobby you choose, what would it be?

If you could have a joint holiday with a set of friends who are also married, who would they be?

CHAPTER 5

Undressing the Soul

*For Christ and the soul are made for one another, and when they are brought
together deep speaks to deep and wounds answer wounds.*
—E. Stanley Jones, English Missionary to India

And the man and his wife were both naked and were not ashamed.
—Genesis 2:25

NAKED BEFORE GOD

The story of human life, as you remember, begins in a garden
paradise. God, creator of all, has finished His world and as
His crowning achievement and glory made man, and woman,
and placed them in the midst of the Garden of Eden. This
garden—filled first with wonders and now filled with wonder-ers—is
the Divine venue where Adam and Eve will encounter one another,
struck by poetic awe in the presence of the other who is like but unlike.
They were both, of course, naked, and the Scriptures tell us that neither
one felt shame at that. The picture of their unhindered intimacy reveals
something of God's sovereign design for all marriages.

The suggestion we have made throughout this book is that intimacy
in marriage is a matter of returning to that unashamed nakedness. And yet,
while it is a relatively simple thing to become shameless in the exposing
of your physical body, it is enormously challenging to live without shame
in the revelation of your innermost person—of your history, your heart,
your mind, and deeper than all these, your spiritual life.

The spiritual aspect of your life reflects the deepest part of who
you are; it is your essence, your core self. We are in our essence *spiritual* beings, composite creatures made by God's own design to possess
body, mind, and soul, and your soul is the part of you that you can

imagine living on after you have died, re-embodied at the resurrection. No person who is known at only one or two of these levels is every truly known. Only the individual who is fully naked is fully known, and if a couple neglects the spiritual aspect of marriage then they commensurately diminish their potential for intimacy.

Intimacy, indeed, is our great desire when coming into marriage. Each person quietly, in the deep recesses of his or her heart, wishes to be known, to be understood, and to be accepted. At the same time, we deeply fear rejection and shame, and so we cover ourselves. The undressing of our souls—which is necessary to experience intimacy—goes against a lifetime of learned covering. Intimacy is hard work.

And yet, spiritual intimacy may well be the most difficult aspect of all to achieve, and we suspect that the difficulty of sharing our spiritual selves lies in our inability to *hide* before God. We can hide before our spouse, hide before our children, hide before friends and coworkers, but when we stand before God we know, implicitly, that no such hiding is possible. When we stand, and speak, and disclose our desires to the Almighty, then we are in a very real way *naked* before Him. Therefore, to share this space with another person—to disclose our spiritual selves to one another, to permit the other to look *in* upon the deepest and most vulnerable recesses of our soul—is to step into a nakedness where pretense, hiding, and self-promotion become impossible. We are letting another person see us undress before God. Nowhere more than in spirituality are we afraid to be naked before others.

This is why it will take special persistence to grow together in the area of spiritual intimacy. It is relatively easy to talk about our interests, hobbies, and family history, but to pray together, to reveal our inmost thoughts about God, to share in matters of faith, these are far more difficult. The kind of sharing asked of us will happen on a level that is well beyond our comfort zones. This difficulty stresses our need for garden walls. All gardens are cultivated, and tended, and all ancient gardens were also walled and protected. Walls in such a spiritual garden provide the safety and security for you to undress yourself without fear.

It is sad that many couples do not believe this area to be very important. Matters of faith and belief in God are considered private, and the assumption is that if you love each other everything will work out. Other couples—where one is a believer and the other is not—deceive themselves into thinking that their spiritual differences are irrelevant, or at least secondary. Quite the opposite, if your spiritual self is your central, deepest self, then your incapacity to share that deepest self with your potential spouse reflects something troubling about your relationship. Not only will you be incapable of being fully known, there is at the outset of your marriage a disagreement about what matters most in the deepest part of your life. Remember, character reveals itself when under distress, and what you believe at your deepest self is what forms your character. Marriage will inevitably bring you to a place of deep personal distress, and if at that point you discover disagreement about what matters most, what will be the outcome? Wiser people believe that spiritual intimacy builds strong marriages. Therefore, cultivate a relationship with your mate that permits you to allow him or her inside the spiritual areas of your life. As you learn to undress spiritually, you will gain a rich harvest of intimacy.

INTIMACY FRACTURED

"It is not good for the man to be alone," says the Lord in Genesis 2:18, the selfsame Being who has just made all of creation and declared it *very* good. The implication is that although the world is God's good work, it is also incomplete. What follows is that God presents Adam with all the animals for him to name, and Adam goes about his work—as we said earlier, noting that each animal has a partner but not he. Naming the animals, then, likely gave Adam insight into his own nature. Something was missing. God creates Eve, and presents her to Adam, and Adam receives a vision for what fulfillment might look like—in the other, someone who is like me but different. And yet, despite God's good plan and our created nature, there remains a deeply ingrained problem with our human pursuit of intimacy. Couples regularly approach marriage with the attitude, whether spoken or unspoken, that "If I marry this person, my life will be fulfilled."

Genesis 3 recounts the reason for this trouble. Adam and Eve, commanded to eat freely from any tree save one, permit the voice of the snake to drown out and sully the voice of God. They eat, and discover they are naked, and hide themselves in shame. The verses that follow give focus to our human struggle for intimacy. God walks in the garden, enjoying the cool of the day, and calls to His children. Knowing something is amiss, God asks Adam what happened, but Adam, rather than fess up, blames Eve (and by extension God, who gave him Eve). Eve in turn blames the snake (and by extension God, who put the snake there). In response, God pronounces His curse upon the woman and man alike.

> To the woman He said,
> "I will greatly multiply
> Your pain in childbirth,
> In pain you will bring forth children;
> Yet your desire will be for your husband,
> And he will rule over you."

> Then to Adam He said, "Because you have listened to the voice
> of your wife, and have eaten from the tree about which I commanded you, saying, 'You shall not eat from it';

> Cursed is the ground because of you;
> In toil you will eat of it
> All the days of your life.
> "Both thorns and thistles it shall grow for you;
> And you will eat the plants of the field;
> By the sweat of your face
> You will eat bread,
> Till you return to the ground,
> Because from it you were taken;
> For you are dust,
> And to dust you shall return."
> —Genesis 3:16–19

Before they had eaten, Adam and Eve were right in their relationship with God, and right in their relationship to the earth (their work), and right in their relationship to one another, and right in their relationship to their inner lives. But after their act of disobedience, all four of these areas were shattered. Our relationship with God is one of *hiding*—we hear His voice and run away. Our relationship with work is frustrated—Adam will cultivate the ground but it will be toil and he will produce thorns; Eve will cultivate children, but the process will also be similar toil and pain. Our relationship to one another is pained as well—Eve's desire will be for her husband and he will *rule* over her—their partnership is fractured. (We can only imagine the conversations that follow for the duration of their marriage: *"You* ate first!" *"You* didn't say anything about it!") Lastly, Adam and Eve are broken within themselves—they experience shame in their innermost person.

Adam and Eve move from right relationship with God, their inner selves, the earth, and one another, to fractured relationships at each of these levels, and into a shame at all of them. Where there is shame such as this, there cannot be intimacy. The process of hiding has begun, and in their footsteps we have inherited a pattern of covering ourselves from exposure to our own shame.

It is noteworthy that this passage also identifies some of the coping strategies to which men and women turn to alleviate our relational discomfort. Frustrated with marriage, men are often tempted to look outside for fulfillment—to their work—and yet their work will be cursed. Women, similarly frustrated, often turn to children for fulfillment—and yet their experience will be marked more by pain than comfort. The result is that while marriage is fulfilling, ultimately it doesn't fulfill. Children are fulfilling, but ultimately they don't fulfill. A career is fulfilling, but ultimately it doesn't fulfill. And none of our strategies for fulfillment can or will satisfy our need for fulfillment, not only because we are cursed, but because we are simply not designed to experience fulfillment in these places.

Only God fulfills, and if you enter into marriage expecting fulfillment from your partner you have set him or her up for inevitable failure.

E. Stanley Jones, missionary to India, writing about the apostle Paul's missionary heart, once said the following,

> He let Jesus commend himself to every man's conscience, for he knew that Jesus appeals to the soul as light appeals to the eye, as truth fits the conscience, as beauty speaks to the aesthetic nature. For Christ and the soul are made for one another, and when they are brought together deep speaks to deep and wounds answer wounds.[26]

The soul is designed to be answered by God. In St. Augustine's words, "Lord, You have made us for Yourself, and our hearts are restless until they rest in Thee."[27] Or as the author of Ecclesiastes writes, "He has also set eternity in [the human] heart" (3:11). There is an insatiable gap in the human heart that only God can fill, and any attempt to fill it by human means will result in disappointment and frustration, and in marriage that disappointment will inevitably affect both you and your partner.

When we turn to another human person to fulfill us, then we set that person to a task they are incapable of filling, if only because the other person is as imperfect as you, if in different ways. You are asking a person to do for you what only God can do, and this programs the relationship for disappointment. Furthermore, when you draw your identity from an imperfect person the effect is to merely copy, and then in time magnify, that imperfection. The only sure means to secure our identity is to ensure that we have grounded it in a *perfect* person. 1 John 4:18 says that "perfect love casts out fear." Perfect love creates the space for true intimacy, and because none of us is capable of loving another person perfectly, we must then draw on the perfect love of God in loving one another.

In this, our love for Christ must take priority in marriage, and our love for spouse a second place. Classically, this is a process called by St. Augustine the *ordo amoris*—the ordering of our loves. We must love those things in proportion to the love they deserve. God first, spouse second, children third, and so forth. Prioritizing the wrong loves means compromising all loves—placing work over children means jeopardizing your relationship with your children. And then what will you have when you retire? Placing your love for your family over that of your spouse means jeopardizing your relationship with your spouse. Placing any relationship over our primary one with God means losing that relationship. Wrongly ordered loves lead to human despair and the failure of intimacy.

When my personal love for God sits in priority over my love for my spouse—where I am cultivating a relationship with God such that I find my ultimate fulfillment in Him—then I can operate in my marriage as a giver rather than a taker. From my deepest life in God, I can become a giver to my partner at the level of my spouse's deepest need. This is also what it means to be the Image of God in the world, because the nature of love, after all, is that it is the giving of self. This truth is at the heart of the Christian faith—God, Triune, is not alone but mysteriously three. Maybe it will help to think of it this way. God is eternal, and God is love. But for love to be complete requires an object for love—you've got to love somebody or something else in order to love. This begs a question—who did God love before the world was created? Put another way, if God *is* love, then how was it that God was able to fulfill His nature when there was no world, and no people, to love? The Trinity provides an answer to this dilemma, because it means that God as Father, Son, and Holy Spirit is able to love within that Triune relationship for all eternity, each member giving Himself in love to the other. God *is* love, love is God's nature, love is how God communicates within Himself to Himself, and we in His image and likeness are creatures made both to love and to be loved. When our soul is secured in God, then we gain access to this eternal, unchanging love. It is this love that we bring as a gift, balm, and boon to our spouse.

SUPERNATURAL LOVE

If we are going to love our spouse with a love from beyond this world, with a truly supernatural love, then (in addition to being

Trinitarian) we will want to consider three other characteristics that mark God's love for us and shape how we view love in marriage. These characteristics each provide opportunities to access the love of God for use in our marriage, but they also provide three critical garden walls that will protect the spiritual heart of your marriage.

The first is that supernatural love is monogamous. The story of God and His people in the Scriptures is the story of a marriage. God calls His people, covenants with them at Sinai, sends John the Baptist as the "friend of the bridegroom" (i.e., the best man), Jesus comes as the groom, and the wedding supper happens at the end of time. The Ten Commandments, in Exodus 20, begin with the language of a marriage covenant:

> You shall have no other gods before Me. You shall not make for yourself an idol, or any likeness of what is in heaven above or on the earth beneath or in the water under the earth. (Exodus 20:3–4)

God enters into a covenant with Israel, and this is a monogamous covenant—one God, one people, joined together for all time. And monogamy for God means, in part, that God is not fickle. He doesn't change His mind. He keeps His promises and commitments. And this is enormously good news for us, because God's perfect love and commitment cannot be compromised even by our infidelity. This is the meaning of God's words in Malachi 3:6, that "I, the LORD, do not change; therefore you, O sons of Jacob, are not consumed." If God changed—if He were to break His marriage covenant with us—then we would be destroyed. It is only God's commitment to His own commitments that keeps us alive. We are thus enabled to draw strength from God's perfect commitment and apply it to our own commitments to one another in marriage.

God's commitment to us, we should note, also informs the strength with which God rejects divorce. If God can put up with our manifold indiscretions, then surely we can put up with one another.

The second characteristic of supernatural love is that it is jealous. We read God's command in Exodus 34:14 that "you shall not worship any other god, for the LORD, whose name is Jealous, is a jealous God." This is a shocking verse to modern ears, but God has claimed that His name, His very reputation, is anchored upon His jealousy. The verse is only shocking because we have largely confused jealousy with greed. The jealous lover today is simply someone who refuses to share their partner with anyone else. But divine jealousy is a measure of your investment in another person. When someone you love is threatened, jealousy is the godly anger that arises in defense of that person. Hence, there are many situations where *not* to feel jealous is wrong! When someone threatens what matters to us, where we have invested our lives, then we ought to experience rising up within us a desire to fight for those things. That desire to "fight for" is jealousy.

We see God fighting for us throughout the Bible. He becomes angry with those places where we trust in things other than Him. He wars against peoples and situations that threaten His chosen people. God's name is Jealous because He is a God who fights in defensive love for His covenant people. We also ought to fight *for* one another. We ought to fiercely protect our investment in one another, to protect our intimacy, to fight off challengers and challenges that threaten the unity and sanctity of marriage. It is tragic that many couples fight *against* one another when they ought to be fighting *for* their marriage. Instead, jealous love ought to draw us side-by-side in unified war against the enemies of our marriages, and to do this we will need to draw upon God's jealous love from the Scriptures.

The third characteristic of supernatural love is that it is forgiving. Isaiah 1:18 says, "'Come now, and let us reason together,' says the LORD, 'Though your sins are as scarlet, they will be as white as snow; though they are red like crimson, they will be like wool.'" God is perfectly committed to us, but we are only ever *imperfectly* committed to Him. God makes up for this gap with forgiveness. This must be so, because no work on our part is capable of bridging the gap between our infidelity to the covenant with God and God's perfect maintenance of it. We live because of forgiveness.

Corrie Ten Boom was a Dutch Christian who was sent to Ravensbruck concentration camp because her family had hidden Jews in their home during the Second World War. After the war, she traveled and spoke about her experiences and testified to God's forgiveness and saving power. On one occasion, after she spoke about God's unlimited forgiveness, a man approached her. He was one of the worst prison guards from the camp where she had been imprisoned! He, not realizing that she recognized him, asked if she would extend God's forgiveness to him. Corrie froze—gripped with incapacity—but as she prayed she chose to obey, and extended her hand in forgiveness. At that moment God's power descended on her, and as "healing warmth seemed to flood my whole being, bringing tears to my eyes" she was enabled to forgive the man and extend God's forgiveness to him personally. In such a moment, when we are incapable of generating forgiveness on our own, we can rely on God's supernatural and forgiving love to one another. And chances are your spouse will never be as wicked as a guard at a concentration camp![28]

CULTIVATING A SPIRITUAL GARDEN

What are some of the key avenues through which you can draw upon this power from God's supernatural strength for your marriage? When it comes down to the day-to-day business of spirituality in marriage, what are some of the practical things you can do to develop spiritual intimacy in your relationship? We want to recommend six tools for cultivating your spiritual garden together.

First, we believe that you should pray together daily as often as you can. You don't need fancy or organized formal prayers. Hold hands each morning before the day begins or evening before going to bed and pray for the day, each other, and any other pertinent things on your hearts. Jerry wakes every morning, makes coffee, takes it to Claudia in bed, and then together they pray for the day. The apostle Peter, in 1 Peter 3:7, advises husbands and wives to live "in an understanding way . . . so that your prayers will not be hindered." When you pray together like this, you come to know another person's heart intimately, and in the process understanding facilitates prayer, while prayer creates the conditions for understanding. As the years go by you will want to add prayers for your children. These prayers don't need to be long. You can talk about things before you pray, but you don't have to. It doesn't need to be one person saying the prayers. You can go back and forth or one person can pray one time, and then another time it could be the other person. The key thing is not to get caught up in rules about this, but strive to make it a natural part of your marriage. And while there will be other times where you might want to pray for world peace, or other people, or other situations, we recommend that you set aside this time to be spiritually intimate. Share your hearts with each other so your mate knows how to pray for you. Start today! It's a great way to feel spiritually connected throughout the day.

Second, spiritually strong couples will incorporate the Scriptures into their life together. This can take a number of forms. Some couples will thrive by reading Scripture aloud together, and this is a wonderful practice with which to begin your new life together. Having a partner to read Scripture with can keep you especially accountable to your daily Bible reading. But you can also set your Scriptural sights in a different place, perhaps choosing one verse each week to memorize together. After 52 weeks you would know 52 verses—and think of the results of that investment over a lifetime together! Again, don't make a work out of this, but feel free to be creative about how you incorporate the Word of God into your relationship.

Third, commitment to a church community is critical for your spiritual sustainability as a couple. Seek out and involve yourselves in a healthy, vibrant church where you can grow both individually and as a couple. If you aren't connected now, there's no better time than now to purpose yourselves to find one. Worshiping side by side, learning together, and serving together breeds a unique flavor of intimacy. Furthermore, a healthy church will provide resources for spiritual direction, growth, and often marriage enrichment. Sermons and homilies can infuse our minds and our hearts with valuable insight to help us grow. Liturgy enriches our spiritual sensitivity. Fellowship with others who are also on a spiritual quest to know God more is a rich resource for counsel and encouragement. You can always find other couples wrestling with the same issues you may be struggling with, and comparing notes about what each of you has learned along the way will only increase your skills as a married couple.

Fourth, finding a place to volunteer together can also enrich your spiritual lives greatly. So much of life is taken up by responsibilities that are demanded from us—work, chores, and so forth. Setting time aside to give freely of your skills and gifts cultivates love and generosity. Jerry and Claudia as well as Liesel and Jeremy, while they were engaged, helped in their church high school programs. We know couples who volunteer in homeless shelters, tutor underprivileged children, or work at summer camps. There are a host of needs and opportunities for you to explore where you can give as a couple. Witnessing your spouse serve others enables you to see not only the love of God working its way through that person, but also to perceive their own unique beauty in a fresh way. So, find a soup kitchen, or a homeless shelter, or an outreach ministry, or a school program, or some other place where you can bless others together and see God work in one another.

Fifth, there is an ancient spiritual practice called the *Examen* that is very simple and can enrich your lives greatly. The *Examen* is a simple exercise where at some point each day, typically near the end, a couple can set aside some time to ask a few simple questions. Where did I feel close to God today? Where did I feel far from God today? Used in youth groups, this is sometimes referred to as "Hi/Lo." But the two simple questions, asked each day, train the mind to reflect daily on the presence of God, and can assist you to discern what God is doing, where you've made missteps, and places you might like to either avoid or return to in the future. This is also a great exercise to bring to your family when it grows, and to mark your family dinners with a short time of reflection each day.[29]

Sixth, a final place to enrich yourselves spiritually is with another ancient practice, pilgrimage. Pilgrimage is a change in your environment that forces you into fresh attentiveness for God. Instead of simply "travel," a pilgrimage demands a special intentionality. Pilgrims are looking for glimpses of God in every adventure. There are big pilgrimages, such as visiting ancient monasteries or the graves of people who have touched your life. There are also simpler pilgrimages, such as visiting your family home or places where you had memorable childhood experiences. The intended benefit of a pilgrimage is that it uses the change in circumstances to force a renewed awareness of God into your ordinary experiences as well. People who become adept at seeking God's presence bring that aptitude with them into everyday life. For three years, Jeremy made monthly pilgrimages to a local monastery where he prayed and restored himself. Jeremy and Liesel, early in their marriage, took a pilgrimage to visit the key sites of Abraham Lincoln in Illinois, including his grave. Jerry and Claudia visited Iona in England. All four of us have been to Gettysburg, Pennsylvania, and experienced the sadness of the memory of such extreme death. Again, the trips don't have to be extravagant to be meaningful and to benefit your everyday outlook as a couple. The key is to ensure that you talk about what's going on inside you while you visit these spaces, and that you listen to what your spouse is experiencing as well. Cultivating such a habit of reflection and response is a critical component of sharing spirituality together on an everyday basis.

Nothing in this list should be taken legalistically. Spirituality is about freedom, not bondage, and you should discuss together which places sound most appealing to you both and seek to incorporate them into your life right now. In a letter to a child who had read his Narnia books, merely a month before his death C. S. Lewis offered her the following advice: "If you continue to love Jesus, nothing much can go wrong with you, and I hope you may always do so."[30] The mutual love of Jesus is the most important thing for your marriage, and what we have found is that as long as each person is growing in their relationship with God by regular Bible study, fellowship, and study with other believers, setting aside specific time together is helpful but not mandatory for spiritual health. In many ways spiritual undressing will happen naturally as long as you both are growing in your personal spiritual life. You will want to ensure, when children come along, that you set aside family time for passing these factors on in order to grow your children's spiritual lives. After all, if practicing spiritual intimacy is habitual for you, you will find it a natural transition to include your children. If you find that you cannot pray together, or cannot read Scripture together without arguing, or that you aren't on the same page spiritually in any way, then these seem to be issues warranting significant discussion *before* you get married.

ASSIGNMENT

Pray together! Set aside some time to discuss those issues that are most critical to you right now. If you're preparing for marriage, try not to allow wedding details to crowd out the other needs of your soul. Listen carefully to one another, and pray *for* one another's felt needs. Try not to "fix" the other person if they share a prayer concern with you, but instead take the opportunity to speak to God on their behalf. Commit to praying *for* one another even beyond your shared prayer time.

PART 2
Unpacking Communication

Chapter 6
Unpacking Gender

Chapter 7
Unpacking Communication

Chapter 8
Unpacking Woundedness

CHAPTER 6

Unpacking Gender

Let me not to the marriage of true minds
Admit impediments. Love is not love
Which alters when it alteration finds,
Or bends with the remover to remove.
—Shakespeare, Sonnet 116

GREAT MYSTERIES

The universe is a vast, immeasurably complex place, full of mysteries beyond the perception of our tiny human minds. Monarch butterflies take a yearly pilgrimage of over 3000 miles and don't lose their way. The moon, between the earth and the sun, is set precisely at a distance where during a total eclipse we can witness the sun's corona. In some regions of the world, every seventeen years a sea of cicadas emerges from the soil to mate, lay eggs, and die off all at once, carpeting the earth with their carcasses. At the biggest level, of planets, stars, solar systems, and beyond, the Law of Gravity is king, ordering the celestial cosmos with perfect regulation. But at the smallest level, beneath even atoms in the region of quarks, the laws of Quantum Mechanics operate. Both sets of laws operate fully. Both sets contradict one another; how the universe runs at the largest level is radically different from how it runs at the smallest. And yet the world does not fall apart, and we continue to breathe air, and in the midst of this great mystery scientists continue to search for a unifying theory that can explain the relationship between the big and the small. The mysteries of the world are innumerable, but perhaps greatest of them to trouble the human mind is the mystery of man and of woman. The book of Proverbs muses about this mystery as follows,

There are three things which are too wonderful for me,
Four which I do not understand:
The way of an eagle in the sky,
The way of a serpent on a rock,
The way of a ship in the middle of the sea,
And the way of a man with a maid.
    —Proverbs 30:18–19

When God made man and woman He chose, for His own good pleasure, to make us in difference, in contrast. He caused us to be made "in His image and likeness," and yet because there are differences we can only conclude that sameness would not have revealed His glory to the same extent. Thus in the genders has been created a poetry of contrasts, an inexplicable harmony between differences, brought together to glorify God in mutual reflection. Unpacking this poetry of the sexes has been the fount of much of our great literature.

Many features make human communication complex and difficult. No two people are exactly alike. We each see from different perspectives and points of view. Our perspectives are influenced significantly by personality, birth order, economic background, education, aptitude, mental capacity, emotional health, physical health, and so forth. But perhaps no feature is more likely to cause miscommunication in marriage than gender. It is here where our limits in communication expose themselves most profoundly.

At heart, we must acknowledge the mystery that men and women are different and perceive the world from different angles of vision. For example, when Claudia was pregnant she would take Jerry's hand and place it on her abdomen so he could feel the child growing and kicking inside her. Jerry would wonder, in amazement, "What is it like to feel another person moving inside one's body?" Such an experience must always remain a mystery to him as a man. Later, when Claudia gave birth to each of their children Jerry watched and thought to himself, "Well, there is something I *never* want to experience!" But when he read the passage of Scripture that says Mary, the mother of Jesus, looked at her newborn son and "treasured these things in her heart," he realized that such a text is immeasurably more proximate to the eyes of a woman than a man.[31] Our wives are better equipped to understand it than we are, precisely because of their gender. On another occasion, after Jerry and Claudia had made love, Jerry asked her, "Do you ever wonder what love-making feels like for a man?" It had never really crossed her mind, but for his part Jerry was very curious what orgasm felt like for a woman. The bottom line is that while we can discuss these matters together, we can never truly know the other person's perspective on life and experiences. Men and women are different—this is a fact. And these differences, say what we may, cannot always be communicated in a way that is understood by the opposite gender with complete success.

ATTEMPTS TO DECIPHER THE MYSTERY

Many have attempted to decipher the differences in gender—some attempts are more successful than others. Overall, however, there appears to be a great deal of head-scratching, humor, and helplessness. Often, attempts to decode gender simply result in caricature. One of the most popular and memorable descriptions was the one offered by John Gray in his book *Men Are from Mars, Women Are from Venus.* The title alone suggests some of the helplessness men and women feel when attempting to communicate with one another! In line with this, it is very popular to identify men as rational and women as emotional. Men are expected to be cool, calm, predictable, and well-reasoned, while women are expected to be more fiery, agitated, unpredictable, and unreasonable. We should observe that our culture, at large, favors the so-called "rational" over the emotional. After all, "Let's be rational" is a very strong argument, while no one ever says, "Let's be emotional about this." In this way, the caricature of men and women implicitly favors men. So, while it is popular to presume that males are rational, logical, and analytical, whereas females are emotional, intuitive, and aesthetic, these caricatures are clearly insufficient. Reason, logic, and the capacity to analyze, as well as emotion, intuition, and an ability to appreciate beauty, are each *human* qualities not strictly identified with one gender or the other.

How do we decode the genders? What is it, at its core, that makes us male and female? Is it only a matter of biology? We want to propose two ways to perceive the differences in gender—one suggests that men and women are assertive vs. nurturing, the other that we are linear vs. networked.

Assertive/Nurturing

When in Genesis 1:27 the Bible declares, "In the image of God he created them; male and female he created them" (NIV), this suggests that there is something of the specifically male as well as the specifically female nature that reflects God's image in the world. Perhaps other Scripture can illuminate this further. For example, when Paul describes his ministry to the Thessalonian church in 1 Thessalonians 2 he writes, in verse seven, that "we proved to be gentle among you, *as a nursing mother* tenderly cares for her own children." Later, in verse eleven, he writes that "you know how we were exhorting and encouraging and imploring each one of you *as a father* would his own children." At least in the apostle Paul's mind, this suggests that the feminine is characterized by its tendency toward nurturing—echoing the gentle care of a mother for her children—and that the masculine by its tendency toward assertiveness—echoed in the language of exhortation, encouragement, and imploring. Our physiology witnesses to this contrast between nurturing and assertiveness as well. In the sex act, the man penetrates—a decidedly assertive act. Additionally, this proclivity toward assertiveness is present in the role that testosterone plays in men's psychology and physiology. By contrast, in sex women are the receivers—the seed is planted within her womb, conception takes place within her body, and it is within her that a child is formed and nurtured. The act of physiological nurturing extends well beyond the sex act, and after birth the woman holds the baby to her breast, where it is weaned and begins to develop. It is likely the defining characteristic of being female that a woman has a natural, biological proclivity toward nurturing.

Linear/Networked

Another way to look at the differences in gender is to see men as "linear" and women as "networked." Men typically have a straightforward, direct approach to the world. They like to think of one thing at a time, and to accomplish one goal before moving on to the next. They are often outward, direct, and driven. Women, however, often have a more lateral approach to the world. They like to think of multiple things at a time, often multitasking, and live within a web of connections. They regularly consider the long-term consequences and complications of a course of actions. A few examples might put this in perspective—men, typically, carry only a wallet, while many women carry purses. With his wallet, the man is confident that he has all he needs for the day, and if he needs something else he'll buy or borrow it. For the woman, the purse is quite simply a bag of possibilities—it prepares for all the contingencies of the day, like tissues, hand sanitizer, gum, water, or whatever else. For Jeremy, it is a relatively simple thing to say to Liesel, "Let's go to the beach today." So long as he has a swimsuit and a towel he's fine. But the moment he makes this suggestion it triggers a whole host of conditions in Liesel's mind—Have I shaved? Do I have sunscreen? Am I on my period? Which swimsuit will I wear? And so forth. What for Jeremy was a simple question (linear), was for Liesel something far more complex (networked).

A linear focus on goals can assist men to perceive and achieve some significant tasks, but it can also eliminate a great deal of beauty along the way. Typically, men who drive on car trips dislike stopping—they want to cover as many miles as possible between stops! It's a very linear way of thinking, but the women in the car are thinking of the next bathroom break—that's a networked way of thinking! One time Liesel and Jeremy were driving through upstate New York on their way to Niagara Falls. Some friends had told them that there was a great little ice cream shop on the way, and Liesel was on the hunt for that little stop. Jeremy was driving fast, passing cars on the two-lane highway and trying to make their destination in good time. All at once, they passed—quickly!—by an ice cream shop on the side of the road. Even at that quick speed, it was clear the shop was closed shut. Jeremy wanted to keep driving on (he had just passed someone!), but Liesel insisted that they at least go back and take a better look. So they pulled to the side (and let the car pass again), and turned around. Slowly pulling up to the ice cream shop, which was obviously closed, Jeremy was inwardly frustrated at the stop in their journey. However, at the exact moment the car came to a stop in front of the shop, the owners rolled up the window and opened business for the day! Jeremy and Liesel both got out and had some great ice cream, but an even better story and reminder that how we see the world enriches one another.

Being linear vs. networked also shows up in communication. Men, when they argue, often focus on the point at hand, while women focus more on relationships (connections). In this way men frequently might win the argument but "lose" their partner in the process, by hurting and being inattentive to her in the process. The communication that worked when he was a man with other men—fighting, arguing, disputing, and debating without relational consequences—must be tempered in communication with his spouse. But for women, for whom everything is connected, when once an argument begins there is a real danger of bringing every other argument in with it. This process is commonly called "kitchen sinking"—throwing every argument into the fray at once.

Are you unconvinced by our hypotheses, and convinced that there are further complexities to be investigated in this area? Have a conversation where you try to decide between the two of you the exact defining characteristics of masculinity and femininity. If you can figure it out, then write the book—you'll make millions! But chances are you won't figure it out completely, and even if you revisit the topic some twenty years after marriage, our guess is that ambiguities will continue to abound. Instead, what makes for successful communication across the gender divide are the factors of patience, trust, and a quickness to forgive and to seek forgiveness whenever misunderstandings occur. The challenges presented by gender are not threats to the success of a marriage; but successful marriages will take into account the complexities and learn skills that reduce the liabilities and maximize the benefits. And keep in mind that the more certain one of you might be to think you have it all figured out the more off-putting it will be to your spouse.

THE WILL

Is one way better than the other? Are there nurturing men and assertive women? Are there linear women and networked men? No, yes, and yes. We are each made in God's image and likeness, and we must remember that each man is 50 percent his mother, while each woman is 50 percent her father. Divisions in gender can illuminate our understanding and bring clarity, but we must not take them to be absolute and binding, and this is because we each have at our disposal access to more than one way of viewing the world. It is only gendered selfishness that refuses the attempt to see from a different perspective. This means that the critical thing to see when we approach one another in communication is that neither of our dominant, or preferred, means of communication provides the basis of communication in marriage. In fact, it is a third thing that is the true basis of all communication in marriage—the will.

Let's return again to the most common caricature of men's and women's thinking—that men are rational while women are emotional. Let's also revisit the idea that our culture at large privileges the rational. "Try to think rationally about this" is a highly effective argument. But the truth of the matter is that reason may in fact be the weakest of our mental faculties. When I want to do something I am very skilled at inventing *reasons* for why I should do it. Some years ago Liesel and Jeremy were still watching their tube television while HDTVs were first becoming commonplace. At that time, it was very easy for Jeremy to invent any number of reasons why he ought to purchase a new television—picture quality, longevity, the old picture wasn't as good, it was smaller and took up less space, and so forth. But none of these "reasons" could overcome the fact that they didn't have the money for one. Instead, reason—and being "rational"—was operating in the service of desire.

Alternatively, how many times can you remember purchasing something simply because it would "feel good"—buying a dessert because "you deserved it," or going on a trip because you needed a break, or standing in line at a store and buying anything at all on impulse. In these scenarios, we have marshaled our emotions to justify our actions on the ground that it will make us feel better.

So, upon reflection, neither reason nor emotion is particularly trustworthy—neither the traditionally male dominant way of thinking, nor the traditionally female dominant way of thinking. But there is a third faculty, shared by both men and women in equal measure, and beyond reason and emotion it is this faculty that has the power to bridge our gaps in communication. This faculty is the will.

The will operates in power over both reason and emotion. It is by the will that a person can reenter a burning building to rescue someone. Confronted with fire, reason says, "Pain hurts, and death is real. You should choose to live. Don't do it." Confronted with burning, the emotions say, "Ouch! Fear! Run away!" But the will can override both of these and risk your life to save someone else's. A marriage, in much the same way, is fundamentally a matter of the will. When you stand before God and marry another person, you are doing so by employment not of your reason ("Marrying her is a good choice because of the benefits I receive"), nor of your emotion ("I love the way I feel around him and want to feel this way forever"), but of your will—"I choose to stay with you no matter what for the remainder of my natural life."

Shakespeare writes, in Sonnet 116, that "Love is not love / Which alters when it alteration finds." These words paint a picture of the will that is love, and love that is will. The rest of the sonnet is worth review as well:

> Let me not to the marriage of true minds
> Admit impediments. Love is not love
> Which alters when it alteration finds,
> Or bends with the remover to remove.
> O no! it is an ever-fixed mark

That looks on tempests and is never shaken;
It is the star to every wand'ring bark,
Whose worth's unknown, although his height be taken.
Love's not Time's fool, though rosy lips and cheeks
Within his bending sickle's compass come;
Love alters not with his brief hours and weeks,
But bears it out even to the edge of doom.
    If this be error and upon me prov'd,
    I never writ, nor no man ever lov'd.[32]

Love is unchanging—it is a function of the will!—it is unshaken, unaltered by time, unaffected by circumstance, and unfazed by changes even in the beloved. The loving will, in action in a marriage, compensates for the differences presented in gender through a reapplication and rededication to commitment. This has direct impact on our communication because, again, neither reason nor emotion is best. Neither the male dominant nor the female dominant mode of communication is perfect. In fact, whatever may be our preferential modes of communication, they simply form two sides of a triangle, the third of which is the will, and this is the faculty you each possess in equal measure. Communication across the gender divide, then, is an ongoing choice, and the will is the faculty that has power to bypass many of the complications produced by gender. It is the common ground where our souls encounter one another in marriage.

GENDER AND THE SCRIPTURES

Given all this, we ought to note how Ephesians 5, commonly considered one of the most difficult passages in the New Testament about gender relations, targets the will and calls for its sanctification. This is a deeply unpopular word to hear, not least because of the uncomfortably un-twenty-first-century appeal to submission directed at wives. But a closer reading reveals deep insights into the human heart. Consider the first portion of the apostle Paul's difficult words now,

Wives, be subject to your own husbands, as to the Lord. For the husband is the head of the wife, as Christ also is the head of the church, He Himself being the Savior of the body. But as the church is subject to Christ, so also the wives ought to be to their husbands in everything.

—Ephesians 5:22–24

These words are clear—almost regrettably so! There is a distinct call to submission and indeed subjection that is made specifically to women in the text. We've even looked up the Greek word translated "in everything" in verse 24. The word is *panta*, and it does indeed mean *all things*. Wives are to subject themselves to their husbands in the same way that the church subjects itself to Christ.

If the passage ended there, I expect it would be intolerable, but Paul goes on to give instruction to husbands as well. We might observe that while Paul takes only three verses to explain things to the wives, he takes three times as many to explain things to the husbands! He writes,

Husbands, love your wives, just as Christ also loved the church and gave Himself up for her, so that He might sanctify her, having cleansed her by the washing of water with the word, that He might present to Himself the church in all her glory, having no spot or wrinkle or any such thing; but that she would be holy and blameless. So husbands ought also to love their own wives as their own bodies. He who loves his own wife loves himself; for no one ever hated his own flesh, but nourishes and cherishes it, just as Christ also does the church, because we are members of His body. FOR THIS REASON A MAN SHALL LEAVE HIS FATHER AND MOTHER AND SHALL BE JOINED TO HIS WIFE, AND THE TWO SHALL BECOME ONE FLESH. This mystery is great; but I am speaking with reference to Christ and the church. Nevertheless, each individual among you also is to love his own wife even as himself, and the wife must see to it that she respects her husband.

—Ephesians 5:25–33

If you missed it, review verse 25 for a moment. Husbands are to love their wives *as Christ loved the church*. How again did Christ love the church? Didn't he *die* for it? And with this we see that the call to submission from Ephesians 5 is not a bargain for husbands—the submission of your wife comes at a cost, the cost of your life. If you possess by virtue of your gender a God-given authority in marriage, therefore, it is authority that is grounded in your complete and self-sacrificing love for your spouse. Anything less than that is both tyrannical and un-Christlike.

We should note, then, that both the call to submission and the call to self-sacrifice are summonses directed at the will—both to the selfish will that despises the idea of self-subjection, and to the selfish will that despises the idea of self-sacrifice. Is it possible that these summonses are directed at a deeper understanding of our gendered nature? Adam, cursed, will look outside of marriage for fulfillment—but God commands men to lay down their lives for their spouses. Self-serving men must become self-sacrificing men. Eve's curse declares that her desire shall be for her husband, and yet she must choose to submit as well— pride made to surrender and bow for the sake of love. Perhaps, then, we might see how here in the mutual summonses to submission and self-sacrifice marriage effects a sanctification of the will. The mandate for marriage hits us where we hurt.

No small kerfuffle has arisen over how to interpret this passage (and others like it). Broadly, of course, there are two camps of disputants—"complementarians" (who hold that there is an order to the genders) and "egalitarians" (who hold that the genders are equal). We don't believe you have to choose (or even identify with) a particular camp to have a successful marriage, so long as you acknowledge the complexities of gender, discuss them together, and are striving to love one another sacrificially according to the command of Scripture.

However, a few brief comments into the debate might be worth making. One is about authority, and the other about "headship." It seems clear that much of the disagreement between these two camps arises from the question of "Who's in charge?" When it comes to authority, we ought to remember that all true authority is given, not inherited, and that all authority in relationships is derived from love. You will possess, and gain, authority over people to the degree that you love them. Christ, who gave his life for the world, also inherits all authority over the world. If, in love, the wife is submitting to her husband in all things, and if, in love, the husband is sacrificing his life for his wife's benefit in Christ, then your mutual submission will be so rich that to the outside observer *nobody will be able to tell who is in charge.* In fact, it will be clear to all who see that, in obedience to the dictates of Ephesians 5, Christ is the one who is in charge of your marriage. The model for biblical headship, faithfully followed by both husband and wife, therefore puts Jesus in the command seat of every marriage.

Headship is the second issue, and C. S. Lewis offers the following interpretation of this issue in *Mere Christianity,*

> The need for some head follows from the idea that marriage is permanent. Of course, as long as the husband and wife are agreed, no question of a head need arise; and we may hope that this will be the normal state of affairs in a Christian marriage. But when there is a real disagreement, what is to happen? Talk it over, of course; but I am assuming they have done that and still failed to reach agreement What do they do next?

> They cannot decide by a majority vote, for in a council of two there can be no majority. Surely, only one or other of two things can happen: either they must separate and go their own ways or else one or other of them must have a casting vote. If marriage is permanent, one or other party must, in the last resort, have the power of deciding the family policy. You cannot have a permanent association without a constitution.[33]

To put this another way, in a corporation decision making is made by majority, and the boards in those corporations are always composed of an odd number to prevent a tie vote. But how do you resolve a split vote in a corporation of two, such as marriage? In part, headship might mean that if a husband and wife have a major decision before them and they do not see eye to eye, the final casting vote goes to the husband. This must be done, of course, with obedience to Ephesians 5 in mind—that the decision is made self-sacrificially and for the glorification of the spouse. In such a circumstance, couples would also be wise to exhaust all other options first. They ought to pray together about the decision, gather all possible data so that they can make the best possible decision, seek counsel from others as necessary and appropriate, and delay the decision until the last possible moment. But if that moment for the decision comes and the two of you are still not in agreement, the only options are to either dissolve the union (divorce), or grant one partner to have the deciding vote. The Scriptures indicate that this vote falls to the man. In such a situation, it would also be wise to consider which partner will be required to bear the greatest burden in view of the decision, and to favor that individual's input accordingly.

If the Ephesians 5 passage becomes an issue of contention or demand every day or every week, or perhaps every year in a marriage, this is probably—in a healthy marriage—far too frequent and indicates a level of dysfunction in the relationship. Speaking from the experience of over forty years of marriage, for Jerry and Claudia the exercise of this headship clause has only come up six times in their marriage, and Jerry is happy to report that of those six times, three of them he was right! Of course, that means the other three times he was wrong! In those three circumstances, making the decision and getting on with things moved them past the point where they had been stuck. Then, as incoming data revealed that a wrong decision had been made, for two of those three wrong decisions they were able to go back and set it right. Headship, then, can never be exercised apart from humility, and you will only be "right" in your decisions when it is right for your marriage as a whole.

ILLUMINATE ONE ANOTHER

As we close this section on gender, let's once again recall Chesterton's maxim that "The world will never starve for want of wonders, but only for want of wonder." With that in mind, resist the urge to box your spouse into a category of gender that limits his or her ability to surprise you. Instead, conversations about gender provide opportunities for mutual wonder and illumination, and we are convinced that it can become an area of ongoing and enriching personal growth to learn from one another's gendered perspectives on life. Not only, then, are you challenged to engage in an ongoing conversation about gender, but you are also invited to permit your spouse to bring his or her uniquely gendered perspective to bear upon your own. Gender, in other words, offers an opportunity for mutual illumination.

Jerry, once, in the midst of a discussion with Claudia, asked her, "What does it feel like for you when you are approaching the time of your period?" She answered, "I feel like I want to climb right out of my skin." Jerry was amazed to hear this—and while he's sure he still doesn't know *exactly* what she meant, in response he exclaimed to her, "Why, that's exactly how a man feels about his sexual desire most of the time; he feels the desire so strong that he wants to climb right out of his skin!" She was equally surprised to hear this and the ensuing conversation brought much light—and we hope—much understanding that has been helpful over the years.

At one point in their marriage, Liesel read *Boundaries* by Henry Cloud and John Townsend and resonated with its contents. In an opening chapter, the authors describe a day in the life of a person who struggles with boundaries, and Liesel felt as if they were describing her life! She asked Jeremy to read a chapter so that he could better understand her, and when Jeremy read that opening chapter, his overwhelmingly incredulous thought was, "Why would *anyone* live like this?" It was difficult for Jeremy to step inside the inner life of Liesel at that time (and still is!), but it was an important step in discovering that she saw and experienced the world in a much different way than he did. The point, in both of these cases, is that an attempt to communicate across the gender divide brought some clarity and certainly some sympathy one for the other.

Ignoring this process of mutual illumination cultivates ignorance and can generate wounds, and an example from Jerry's pastoral experience illustrates this. It is common for people to come to their pastor to unburden their heart with any manner of personal concern. Over time, pastors get to hear just about everything one could imagine. In the process you learn to take each person seriously, and to keep confidences so that individuals will be willing to unburden themselves. On one occasion a woman came to Jerry's office and said she was deeply troubled about her son. Asking her what the trouble was, she told Jerry that she feared her son was perverted sexually. This was, to be clear, a deeply amusing suggestion, because her son was still an infant. But keeping his face perfectly serious he asked her in response, "What would lead you to believe something like this since your son is only 18 months old?" She responded, "I believe my son is sexually deviant because nearly every morning when I go to change his diaper he has an erection."

Jerry managed to keep from laughing at her lack of knowledge as he explained to her, simply, that all boys and men will occasionally have erections in the morning, and that it has nothing to do with sexual desire. In fact, it is merely a feature of male anatomy. It stands to follow that she and her husband had never discussed these matters, and consequently it was affecting how she was treating her infant son. It is likely that she only took notice of her husband at times when he was sexually aroused, and therefore deduced that such anatomical changes only occurred during sexual arousal. Her universalized, and misguided, judgment led her to misunderstand her child in a most serious manner.

How else could this mother have learned about these matters? They would not be intuitively available to her, and her own gender would prevent her from knowing *insider* information about her husband and his gender. Therefore, unless attempts to communicate about matters of gender are at least *attempted* we are left with serious liabilities such as these. And yet the effort ought not to be a burden, because there is potential for the curious-minded to achieve a lifelong fascination and wonder concerning these things. And while misunderstandings are inevitable, the creative, empathetic couple will find many ways to navigate these differences, each to the other's mutual benefit.

ASSIGNMENT . . . .

Have a conversation about gender together:

What do you think marks the key differences between the genders?

What do you think are the special strengths and weaknesses of each gender?

Do you identify at all with the categories of assertive/nurturing or linear/networked?

How do you respond to the summons to submission outlined in Ephesians 5?

Can you think of something you wish your partner knew about your uniquely gendered body?

CHAPTER 7

Unpacking Communication

And so these men of Indostan,
Disputed loud and long,
Each in his own opinion
Exceeding stiff and strong,
Though each was partly in the right,
and all were in the wrong!
—John Godfrey Saxe, "The Blind Men and the Elephant"

A TANGLED MESS

*I*n John Godfrey Saxe's poem "The Blind Men and the Elephant," six blind men offer their best insights into the nature of an elephant they are examining. One falls against the elephant's side and declares that it is like a wall. Another grasps the tusk and declares that the elephant is like a spear. The third grasps the trunk and declares the elephant to be like a snake. As the poem concludes the men dispute loud and long, entrenched in their own perspectives and refusing to understand the perspective of the others.[34] The poem is an entertaining study in how sometimes we can be blinded by our own perspectives, and it illustrates clearly some of the key difficulties of communication in marriage.

How do we, after all, come to terms with our differences? How do we learn to resolve the innate differences in perception that originate in our gender? How are we supposed to fight? What does agreement look like? How do we recover when we've been wounded? On their own, each of these concerns would be significant enough, and yet added to this mixture is our mutual sinful natures, which make a mess of this process. Proverbs 27:15–17 (in addition to offering us evidence that the Bible is a book with an ironic sense of humor) appears to present two stark alternatives in communication:

A constant dripping on a day of steady rain
And a contentious woman are alike;
He who would restrain her restrains the wind,
And grasps oil with his right hand.
Iron sharpens iron,
So one man sharpens another.

Two statements, side-by-side, that couldn't be more different. The wife is compared to a constant drip wearing down her husband by means of a kind of Chinese water torture of nagging. Compared to this is the iron that can, through conflict, sharpen iron. We are left to wonder which kind of communication best characterizes our marriages—will we be nagging drips to one another, or will our iron serve the purpose of mutual sharpening? Neither process promises to be comfortable, and the truth of the matter is that while sinfulness and fractured relationships affect us all, it is nowhere more than in marriage that these fractures expose themselves. Communicating with one another in marriage forces us like no other experience to encounter the limits of our own life-experience.

The reason why this is the case is because communication in marriage is vastly different from communication with the rest of the world. Consider that often, when you take your car to the local drive-thru restaurant, the conversation that takes places between you and the associate on the other end of a raspy speaker is frustrating. You will be required to repeat your order more than once. There will be confusion. You will say the words, "I want chicken nuggets" and to your great mystification the associate will respond, "So you want a hamburger, right?" Frustration can mount to such a degree that you might be tempted to offer free advice to the restaurant associate on their suitability for work, or perhaps even their continued existence in society. But when you've got your food and paid your bill, you will drive away from the conversation. You won't be able to drive away from your spouse. Similarly, if while you are sitting at dinner the phone rings and a salesperson wants to sell you a timeshare in the Bahamas, you can snort in disgust, complain about the interruption, and hang up the phone. Case closed. But you'll find that you cannot really snort at, complain to, and hang up on your spouse with the same lasting satisfaction. Or perhaps you have a friend with whom you experience some disagreement—about politics, or an insult, or something else. When it comes to the friendship, you can distance yourselves and take a break for a week or two to cool off and reset—but this very night you're going to be sharing a bed with your spouse!

Communication in marriage is different from communication with the world because, unlike the world, you cannot ignore your spouse, or postpone her, or shut him up. The *closeness* of marriage demands that we make an accounting for different needs in communication. Furthermore, if we are mindful of our covenant status, then taking those words "till death do us part" seriously will mean that the manner of our communication directly affects the happiness of our relationships. We must be extremely mindful of this reality, because there is a great temptation toward discourtesy in communication with one's spouse. We have been implicitly taught that home is where you "let your hair down," that a "man's home is his castle," and that therefore individuals who are weary of keeping up appearances with the world have tacit permission to be rude, insensitive, and selfish when at home. This is false, and in many ways the summons to courtesy ought in fact to be higher with one's spouse than it is with one's friends, coworkers, and associates.

The bottom line is that communication is hard, and communication between sinners is even harder, and communication with your sinful spouse is likely to be hardest of all. How can we best learn to navigate these innate difficulties in marriage?

CONFLICT AND COMMUNICATION IN PERSPECTIVE

To begin, let us attempt to place our expectations about communication in proper perspective. One expectation that is false but commonly held is the idea that all conflict is problematic. Quite the opposite, **having no conflict is not the sign of a healthy marriage.**

Pause, and read that once again—a lack of conflict is *not* the sign of a healthy marriage. In Genesis 2:24 the first marriage is described as a *leaving* of mother and father, and a *cleaving* to one's spouse. It would be naïve to assume that such cleaving—the forcible unification of two personalities—will not be attended by a measure of discomfort. That discomfort is conflict. Again, if Proverbs 27:17 accurately describes a goal for our communication, then as my spouse's iron sharpens me I will experience discomfort—sometimes grating, repeated discomfort—in the process of being honed for better use.

What might be a startling truth of communication, about which many people are misinformed, is the fact that agreement is not the sign of successful communication. Simply because two people agree on everything does not indicate that each person has successfully voiced his or her concerns, desires, or feelings on a given subject. As William Wrigley, founder of Wrigley's gum and former owner of the Chicago Cubs, once wrote, "When two men always agree, one of them is unnecessary."[35] Your spouse is not called to be a "yes-man" or a rubber-stamp to your particular desires in marriage. Quite the opposite, your spouse's vocal disagreement may be precisely the iron that sharpens your dullness, the "rebuff," in Browning's poem again, "that turns earth's smoothness rough." Seen this way, conflict is a process that alters our preconceptions, offering nuance to complexity, and enriching our final conclusions. Such an invitation echoes C. S. Lewis's thoughts about the importance of exposing ourselves to alternative perspectives in literature. He wrote,

> My own eyes are not enough for me, I will see through those of others. Reality, even seen through the eyes of many, is not enough. I will see what others have invented. Even the eyes of all humanity are not enough. I regret that the brutes cannot write books. Very gladly would I learn what face things present to a mouse or a bee; more gladly still would I perceive the olfactory world charged with all the information and emotion it carries for a dog.[36]

And yet it is important to stress that conflict is not a destination. We are not meant to live in a state of conflict, but to traverse conflict as a kind of bumpy road on the way to understanding. It is understanding that is the purpose and goal of all communication in marriage, and conflict ought to be bounded in marriage to its usefulness in facilitating that journey to fresh, deeper, mutual understanding. What this means is that successful communication in marriage is measured not by the amount of conflict, so much as the manner of it. It is not *that* you argue, but *how* you do it that matters most. A few diagrams may help to clarify this further.

Hot/Volatile

Cold/Placid

Many people assume that the best metric of conflict is whether it is "hot" or "cold"—that is, whether a given argument is characterized by volatility or a placid temperament. But indicators of the temperature of a given communication, we are learning, are inadequate measures of actual communication. This recognition comes in part from some of the research done by Dr. John Gottman and recorded in his book *The Seven Principles for Making Marriage Work*.[37] Gottman, a psychiatric researcher, had performed extensive studies on marital communication and developed a set of metrics that allowed him to predict the likelihood of divorce with 91 percent accuracy after watching a mere five minutes' footage of a couple conversing. One of the key factors that appeared in those recorded conversations was contempt. Contempt is a universally recognized human emotion, represented in facial expressions by something as simple as an eye roll. It communicates, nonverbally, both the superiority of one partner and the dismissal of the other. Instead of inviting communication, contempt closes communication. Its presence in communication alters our perceptions of what matters most in communication, so we might consider a second diagram below, containing an alternative axis:

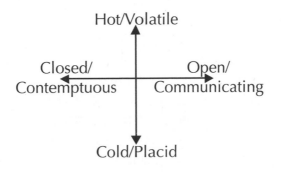

What determines your success in communicating with your spouse is not whether you are hot or cold, but whether you are open or closed, contemptuous or communicating. This further suggests that a couple can be engaged in a knock-down drag-out fight, with raised voices and rapid pulses, but so long as they remain open they can be successfully communicating. Alternatively, a couple might be perfectly placid, with no fight in sight, but be as closed as a vault door to one another, quietly bearing deep contempt toward one another. This means that successful communication is measured not by heat, but by openness, not by the fact of an argument, but the manner in which you conduct it.

UNMASKING THE SEEDS OF CONTEMPT

Before we discuss those elements that establish good habits of communication, let's take a few minutes more to explore the various ways that contempt poisons our relationships. A first way is through what Gottman calls criticism.[38] There will always be times in marriage when we will need to voice a complaint about our partner: You've made a mess in this room. You've failed to take the trash out. You're running late. Part of the closeness of the relationship will force these kinds of issues inevitably to the surface. But criticism stretches these individual complaints into more generalized statements about the person in question. "This time you've made a mess" becomes, "You're *always* making messes." "You've failed to take the trash out" becomes "You *never* take out the trash." "You're running late" becomes "You're *always* running late." We might note the role that words like *always* and *never* play in these kinds of statements. Instead of lodging a complaint (which you ought to be able to do), you are now offering a statement about your partner's character. Instead of saying, "This issue bothers me and I'd like to fix it," you are suggesting through your language and tone of voice that, "*You* are a messy person; *You* are negligent in your chores; *You* don't care about time." In this way, criticism turns a complaint into an *ad hominem* (an attack against the person), and transforms a specific issue into a broad label. By thus painting your partner with an unfair brush you effectively close him or her off to further communication.

The second seed of contempt is physical contempt itself. Remember, the universally recognized facial expression for contempt is an eye roll—people in every culture acknowledge and recognize this expression in the same way that they recognize anger, happiness, or sadness. What contempt conveys to your partner is your personal disgust at his or her behavior, statements, or existence. Contempt emotionally accuses your partner of being unworthy of consideration. When you express it, you are saying through your body language, "What you have to say, what you think, and in fact who you are, these things disgust me." A wise couple will learn to carefully monitor this emotion and the body language that accompanies it.

The third seed of contempt is defensiveness, which Gottman describes as "a way of blaming your partner."[39] In defensiveness, we turn our partner's complaints and criticisms back on them. "Well, I wouldn't make so many messes if you were around more often!" "I would take the trash out, but I've been busy making money so that you can have a home to live in!" "I wouldn't be so late if you didn't rush me all the time!" Whatever the issue may be, in defensiveness the couple is no longer speaking about the main issue, but are trading accusations of blame. Our spouse then responds, not to the issue, but to the place where he or she feels personally maligned. As a consequence, the discussion never settles on the matter of real irritation and in time leads each partner to feel marginalized, attacked, wounded, and unheard. Defensiveness in operation thus marks a refusal to accept your partner's attempts at communication. Perhaps one partner is simply offering a complaint about life—some issue that needs to be dealt with in the everyday press of marriage—but defensiveness shuts down the conversation. In time, you might even learn not to offer complaints, because your partner always finds a way to assign the blame back to you. This throws a forbidding roadblock up to successful communication.

These seeds of contempt offer insight into one of Jesus's teachings from the Sermon on the Mount—or, rather, the Sermon on the Mount offers insight into our understanding of contempt. Consider what Jesus says in Matthew 5:21–24,

> You have heard that the ancients were told, 'YOU SHALL NOT COMMIT MURDER' and 'Whoever commits murder shall be liable to the court.' But I say to you that everyone who is angry with his brother shall be guilty before the court; and whoever says to his brother, 'You good-for-nothing,' shall be guilty before the supreme court; and whoever says, 'You fool,' shall be guilty enough to go into the fiery hell. Therefore if you are presenting your offering at the altar, and there remember that your brother has something against you, leave your offering there before the altar and go; first be reconciled to your brother, and then come and present your offering."

A critical phrase to interpret this passage is found in verse 23, where we read that the situation Jesus describes here is for when "your brother has something against you." In other words, the advice in this passage is targeted to when I am in the wrong. With that in mind, we can review the rest of the passage with fresh illumination, because my anger with my brother, my dismissal of him as a good-for-nothing, and my labeling of him as a "fool" (or empty-head), each of these is predicated on my being in the wrong. He has uttered a complaint, and I have become defensive, and contemptuous, and critical of him, and Jesus says that permitting these seeds of contempt to grow in my heart are as bad as committing a murder. Contempt, in other words, murders our relationships. We must be diligent instead to put *it* to death.

ESTABLISHING THE HABITS OF COMMUNICATION

Where criticism, contempt, and defensiveness operate in full and ongoing force, Gottman has found that marriages will rarely survive. To counteract these dangers, however, we can practice a number of good habits in communication that fall under three big headings: Honesty, Friendship, and Grace.

Honesty

Honesty in communication points to a fundamental disposition: each partner in an honest marriage will be doing his and her part to see the relationship as it really is, and to see your partner, and his or her complaint, for what *it* really is. In some ways, then, honesty might rightly be seen as a synonym for humility. It acknowledges the limits to my own understanding and the reality that, in any given circumstance, there are many things I don't know. An honest disposition in communication will therefore begin with what is known and seek to understand what is not known. The byproduct of such a commitment is that judgments must be softened until, in any situation, as much information as is possible can be grasped. By contrast, dishonest couples paint situations to their preferences, and weigh the scales improperly in their own favor. In this way, we might identify two key components to honesty in communication: impartiality and perspective.

We must acknowledge that in no discussion is either partner ever truly neutral—there are no Switzerlands in marriage from which one partner can deal objectively with the concerns of the other. Instead, because with every discussion each partner is invested in a position, couples ought to strive to be impartial. Impartiality is defined as "the inclination to weigh both views equally." To comprehend this better, imagine for a moment that a husband and wife, during a discussion, have a balance scale set between them. Impartiality means that each argument is weighed fairly, and justly, and that there are no added weights or measures to distort the outcome. When I fail to be impartial I am dishonest because I am distorting my interpretation and presentation of events in order to maximize my benefits and limit yours. After all, each of us operates in life under a set of assumptions that are framed by our life experiences, our personalities, things we've read and learned, previous encounters with other people, and so forth. Each of these factors generates our perspective, which is never neutral—it is *ours*. Although we functionally operate in life under these assumptions, sometimes we fail to recognize that they are incomplete. Thus, from partial information, we project our imperfect understanding onto others. This is one of the key ways that we weigh the scale in our own favor. Contrary to this, with impartiality I make a commitment to give full consideration to the opinion of my partner. I want to hear and understand it fully, in all of its implications, before making a judgment. I will make the effort to see a situation through my partner's eyes.

This dovetails into the second aspect of honesty, which is found in *perspective*. To employ another picture, perspective in communication is an invitation to draw as big a circle as possible around a given issue. What often happens in marital discussions is that the couple becomes fixated on a single issue. This fixation can lead to an incapacity to take in better information, to see things from our partner's perspective, or to grasp the wider implications of what is at stake. Drawing a big circle widens our data set, and offers us a fresh vantage point from which to make a judgment about a given situation. When a couple steps far enough back from a given problem, it can provide them with an opportunity to reassert their commonalities as well.

One of the key ways this works in marriage is by giving "veto power" to our spouse over our impressions of their point of view. In other words, my spouse is the only person who can confirm if I have accurately understood his or her opinion on a given matter. By giving her "veto power," I enable her to correct my misunderstanding and to reattempt to communicate with me. Actively engaging in this process generates a kind of dance in communication, a back-and-forth of "did I get it yet?"

There are often surprising results for both parties, and as a matter of course, you are likely to find that some of your biggest arguments are not what, on the surface, they appear to be about. Sometime during Jeremy and Liesel's first months of marriage the Winter Olympics were happening. They purchased a pair of rabbit ears (an early television antenna!) in order to pick up the local signal. This small event snowballed into a huge fight between them. Why? Jeremy preferred not to have a television signal in the house at all, and became belligerent in expressing his displeasure. This, in turn, irritated Liesel, who just wanted to watch the Olympics in peace. At first, the disagreement centered on the relative merits of television, commercials, and the use of time. But as they attempted to listen more closely to one another, some different perspectives emerged. Jeremy would say, "Why do you love television so much?" And Liesel would say, "I don't love television." Jeremy would try again, "Commercials are such a waste of time—why do you want to waste your time this way?" And Liesel would say, "I'm not wasting my time." It took about a week of back and forth before they reached clarity. In the process, they discussed how television had functioned in their respective homes, and after a certain point Liesel was finally able to say, "Jeremy, you have a way to rest by watching movies and playing games, but I don't have that." The argument, in other words, was not about television so much as it was about *rest*. Until Jeremy was able to understand this, and repeat it back to Liesel, communication had not been effective.

Such a new perspective brought new clarity to the argument. It helped them to finally understand the real nature of their discussion. Engaging in the process gave Liesel time to articulate what was really in her heart. Seeing things through Liesel's perspective helped Jeremy to soften his arguments and to begin to advocate for his wife's desire for rest. Their new clarity helped them to navigate their way through the disagreement. Implicit in the call to seek perspective is a similar summons to *patience*. We are none of us particularly adept at communicating our deep desires and feelings, and sometimes we require time to articulate those deeper aspirations. Impartiality and perspective, by keeping us honest, help to create the space where one partner can grow in speaking from the heart to the other.

This process will be helped along immeasurably if you will make it a habit to assume, for a given conversation, that your assumptions regarding your spouse's perspective are wrong, or at least will always require adjustment. The first assumption, when we hear something from our partner that doesn't ring quite right to us, must be to assume that we have misunderstood. If you begin from the perspective that your spouse is at fault (weighing the scale against him or her!), then this is a recipe for unnecessary conflict. Take a moment to reformulate your spouse's words in your own mind, then repeat them back to him or her and ask for confirmation, "Is this what you mean?" This is the point when you are giving veto power over your impression. Should your partner respond to your characterization of what was said with a statement such as, "No, I didn't mean that at all," be grateful that you did not react based on your faulty first impression.

Baron Friedrich von Hügel, an influential philosopher of religion and spiritual director, once wrote the following,

[N]othing in philosophy, still more in religion, should ever be attempted in and with the first clearness (what, e.g., journalists are content with, and have to be content with), but in and with the *second clearness*, which only comes after that first cheery clarity has gone, and has been succeeded by a dreary confusion and obtuseness of mind. Only this second clearness, rising up, like something in no wise one's own, from the depths of one's subconsciousness—only this is any good in such great matters. And this process is costly, humiliating, and very easily disturbed by rubbishy self-occupations.[40]

This is an invitation, in every important matter, to press beyond our first, simple impressions, and ever more into deeper and more significant clearnesses. Often, we are likely to find that the second clarity is inadequate as well, and then we will need to press into the third and fourth clarity before we have understood the complexity surrounding communication with our spouse. While this process may seem both cumbersome and tedious, given the weight of the discussion it is a vital procedure necessary to ensure that clarity is achieved and civility is practiced. Skill will increase through practice and the process, given time, will become less awkward, will demonstrably reduce defensiveness, and is likely to manifest a real desire to understand one another. It will also at times expose us to perspectives that had never occurred to us. While I may be concerned about A, B, and C, my spouse is invested in X, Y, and Z. Only a big enough circle in perspective can encompass all these concerns and show a good way to navigate the difficulty together.

Friendship

The second habit to establish wholesome communication is friendship. This, in Gottman's estimation, is the single most important factor involved in marital happiness. But friendship is far more than being a buddy with your spouse, it is the active and practiced habit of investing in the other person relationally. A good portion of the work we have suggested in this book so far is meant to build up this kind of friendship. An additional aspect of this kind of friendship is courtesy. The idea of courtesy derives from the "courtly" world of lords and ladies *at court*. It describes the boundaries of civil relationships. In marriage, courtesy prohibits name-calling, proscribes cheap shots, and can prevent couples from spiraling into bitterness. We practice it when we presume the best of our partner's statements, when we speak civilly to one another, when we imagine that each and every sentence spoken is being watched by someone else. Courtesy is not opposed to brutal honesty, or to high emotion, but throughout our marital communication it ought to exhibit itself as an underlying commitment to respect and honor in every discourse. In happy couples, Gottman found that the ratio of positive to negative interactions was five to one. That means that for every negatively experienced interaction with your spouse, you ought to be aiming for five positive experiences. Gottman calls this the "magic ratio."[41]

Courtesy, however, is meaningless—or even insidious—without a disposition of trust. Trust is built from a shared life together, from an accumulation of good experiences, and from character that has been proven over time. Imagine that you agree to meet with a friend every Wednesday morning for prayer and fellowship. These meetings continue for over a year, without break, until one Wednesday morning you show up but your friend does not. Your first reaction in that situation is not likely to be, "That liar! I knew he wasn't trustworthy!" No, because you have established trust, it is far more likely that your first reaction will be to think, "Something must have happened." Trust, over time, establishes goodwill between couples. If one partner returns from work and slams the house door, grumbles while taking off shoes, stomps down the hall, and starts an argument with you, then from the perspective of trust you are likely to assume, "Something must have happened today." Trust in this way accumulates like a bank balance. Periodically, one partner or the other will make a withdrawal, but so long as there is regular input into the account, the relationship will be buoyed by the balance of trust. Many of the types of "undressing" we have discussed in this book are investments in trust.

Friendship in marriage is further advanced by bids, or openness. A "bid" is an effort made by one partner to touch base in the middle of a disagreement. Two people, for example, are discussing some issue quite hotly, arguing back and forth for their own perspectives, but in the middle of the heat the wife reaches out and touches the husband's hand. This is a bid—an effort to reconnect in the midst of contention. In that moment the husband has a choice. He can accept the bid (by taking her hand back and squeezing it), or reject it (by pulling his hand away or ignoring her). If he accepts the bid, he for his part reaffirms the relationship. This is an act of emotional perspective, stepping aside from the heat of the argument to communicate to one another that "I'm still in this *with you*, despite our present difficulty." Gottman describes bids as an act of "turning toward," whether through physical touch, a verbal cue, or humor.[42] It communicates to your spouse the sentiment that "I'm on your side. I'm with you."

When your spouse makes a bid in the middle of a discussion, you may be confronted with a decision. In that moment, you have a choice—do I let go of some of my anger and recommit? Or do I reject this bid for affection and press on to win my argument? Victory, in these circumstances, may not be all that you want; quite the opposite, you might win the argument but lose your spouse in the process. Accepting a bid can occasionally be a surrender of your moral high ground, and yet in the long run it will never be ground you regret forfeiting. In certain circumstances, when your spouse offers a bid you might still be feeling the heat of the discussion too intensely, and you might not be ready to receive the bid. If so, you need to attempt to communicate that to your spouse. You may need a break, or you may need to process your feelings for a little more time. Whatever the reason may be, responsibility falls to you to bid to restore perspective with your spouse.

Importantly, bids during an argument communicate an attitude of openness. Paired with impartiality, they communicate to a partner that your ears, and your heart, remain open to be influenced by his or her perspective. Couples who practice the giving and receiving of bids will be highly successful at navigating their heated discussions.

Altogether, however, one of the most critical aspects of friendship is empathy. Empathy is an activity we perform when we imaginatively enter into the perspective of our partner. Not only do we attempt to understand what he or she *thinks*, we want to have an understanding of how he or she *feels*. Empathy, we should be clear, is not agreement, but it reflects the commitment to see a situation from our partner's emotional perspective. This involves a kind of listening as well. Patrick Lencioni observes in his book *The Five Dysfunctions of a Team* that "most reasonable people don't have to get their way in a discussion. They just need to be heard, and to know that their input was considered and responded to."[43] It is startling to realize, but true, that being heard matters more than getting our way. To be truly heard means that your perspective has been acknowledged, that you as an individual have been validated. The person who can listen in this way has effectively imagined the situation from your perspective. Interestingly, this echoes the language of Hebrews 5:7, where the author writes of Jesus that "In the days of His flesh, He offered up both prayers and supplications with loud crying and tears to the One able to save Him from death, and He was heard because of His piety." Here in view is the Garden of Gethsemane, where Jesus prayed to be relieved from the cross. To that request God said, "no," and yet Jesus was nevertheless *heard*. Being understood mattered more than getting His way.

If you struggle to establish empathy, then Jesus's words from Matthew 7 offer a helpful prescription: Log Surgery. Log Surgery is the business of prioritizing the removal of our own logs prior to dealing with the specks in our neighbor's eyes. When you do this, not only will you be better equipped to actually *see* the speck in your spouse's eye with accuracy and discernment, but because you will be tender from your own surgery you are likely to express greater understanding and kindness in your approach. In this way, Log Surgery combines our disciplines of both honesty and friendship—cementing our complaints in undistorted truth as well as empathy.

Grace

The final area of planting seeds of communication is grace. The Sermon on the Mount again offers instruction on how to communicate in difficult relationships, and in this Jesus tells his disciples, "If someone slaps you on the right cheek, turn to him the other also."[44] This is an invitation to press into relationships, even when they become difficult, and even when the other person wounds you (at least so far as it is possible for you to do so). We should clarify that we don't believe Jesus is advocating for people to stay in relationships that are characterized by abuse. But what is unavoidable is that each of us, because we live in a fallen world, will be recipients of sadness from those we love. If we are honest, then we must also admit that we will each be the *cause* of pain to those we love as well. If we do not learn how to work through these difficult times all relationships will be destined for dissolution as fallout from inevitable conflict. The only real solution is grace.

The book of Ecclesiastes observes, "There is not a righteous man on earth who continually does good and who never sins. Also, do not take seriously all words which are spoken, so that you will not hear your servant cursing you. For you also have realized that you likewise have many times cursed others" (7:20–22). We've all said things about other people, whether to their faces or under our breath, and we've done this while driving, while walking away from a meeting, or while engaged in an argument in the shower. We've taken these incautious words and occasionally spoken them in our relationships as well. Sometimes it's more than a word, but also an act done in a moment of time without consideration to how it might inconvenience the ones we love. What can be done about these when they occur? How might such things be processed in a way that builds a marriage rather than detracts from it?

Unresolved, these episodes can accumulate to an explosive point. Our instructions from the Scriptures, however, taken from Paul's words in 1 Corinthians 13:5, are that a characteristic of mature love is that it "does not take into account a wrong suffered." If I am keeping a ledger of wrongs done to me by my spouse, then in maturity I ought to dispose of the ledger entirely. I cannot keep it like a bill collector, quietly waiting for the moment when I can present the bill on the table with grand and dramatic flourish. For our part, if we would be mature and maturing, how can we work to keep this ledger clear? What will it mean for us to turn the other cheek while staying committed to the relationship?

First of all, we must attempt to see when these hurts are grounded in a simple mistake. Very often, when our partner hurts us he or she is quite unaware of how or what they have done. In this, it is not that the individual was thoughtless or intentionally hurtful; it is far more likely that their choice was made with reference to other situations. But we should be gracious—is it really possible to make every decision in light of every circumstance possible? Is it right to hold your partner to a standard of perfect judgments to which you yourself can never possibly hope to attain? You may feel slighted, but if your partner has committed an honest mistake that is grounded in his or her lack of omniscience, then you ought to forgive and move on. You might imagine that the situation would be different if your partner has maliciously harmed you, but it isn't. In the same way that your partner has harmed you, you have harmed other people. You have also been malicious, and spoken the painful word when you didn't have to, and made life a mess for your spouse. It is equally unjust to hold your spouse to a level of perfection from which you yourself fall immeasurably short. In the same way, you will need to forgive and attempt to move on. This is what it means to turn the other cheek in marriage.

But how will we repair when these difficulties arise, whether grounded in mistakes or malice? We will discuss our anger much more extensively in the next chapter, but for now we must discern when it is that we must confront our partner. If he or she has acted in ignorance and harmed us, then it may be your duty to inform them. If they have acted in malice, then it will be your duty to seek to make it right as well. Either way, your goal should be to select an approach that will produce a positive effect. Don't begin with blame, but strive instead to supply the information about how you experienced the consequences of his or her words or actions. This is best done by telling how you felt with what is called an "I-statement." "I felt sad when you said . . ." or "I felt afraid when you did . . ." or "I felt frustrated when you didn't call to say you would be late for dinner." Framed this way, this kind of information gives the other person an opportunity to hear and understand how his or her act may have affected you. This technique also sets aside the question of motive, which is one of the places where we most commonly misjudge other people—after all, how do we really know what motivates another person? Given how seldom it is that we are absolutely sure of our own motives, how can we be so confident to pronounce judgments upon the motives of others? What we *can* speak about with confidence and authority is our own feelings and how certain actions have affected us. We must practice giving this information to our spouse if we want to prevent such things from happening again, and it is a critical step in ensuring that we do not "keep accounts" with one another in a manner that could devastate the relationship.

It is important as well to follow the I-statement with an "I would like" statement. The "I would like" statement expresses our desire for the future. It gives information to the other person—a kind of bid, if you will—offering a reasonable request for change that considers our needs or preferences. There is of course an ongoing give and take in this process. We offer information and allow another to take it and respond respectfully to it. In this way, "I feel" and "I would like" statements enable us to establish some healthy boundaries in the relationship—boundaries that, by means of establishing a habit of grace, make it paradoxically possible for us to draw closer in intimacy.

C. S. Lewis once said that "In coming to understand anything we are rejecting the facts as they are for us in favour of the facts as they are."[45] Achieving understanding with your spouse in marriage will require you to reject the facts "as they are for you"—to grow in perception, to expand your capacity for new information, and to mature in judgment. Each in its own way, honesty, friendship, and grace will equip a couple to combat the dangers of contempt, and together establish a habit of communication that will enrich their marriage and deepen their emotional life together. Then, when you and your spouse are both looking at the same thing, with the same considerations, you will find that you are communicating with depth, insight, and deep, abiding intimacy.

ASSIGNMENT

Some questions for you to discuss together:

What's an argument that we've had where we failed to communicate? Revisit the circumstances and attempt to practice "veto power" over one another's impressions.

Discuss together what it means to be truly "impartial" in your communication. Can you imagine some ways that this habit could show up in your relationship?

Consider the two charts with hot/cold and open/closed. Where do you think you fall on that axis? Where would you like to be? Which quadrant would make you most uncomfortable?

Pick an issue you disagree about and have a conversation about that issue employing "I feel" and "I would like" statements. After the conversation reflect back on how you feel—were you heard for your perspective?

CHAPTER 8

Unpacking Woundedness

The dullest of us knows how memory can transfigure; how often some momentary glimpse of beauty in boyhood is "a whisper / Which memory will warehouse as a shout."
—C. S. Lewis, quoting his friend Owen Barfield

Sorrow makes us all children again, destroys all differences of intellect. The wisest knows nothing.
—Ralph Waldo Emerson

SELF-KNOWLEDGE, AN ELUSIVE IDEAL

*I*f you want to know what you look like, the best place to turn is probably a mirror. There, in the glass, you will be able to take stock of your appearance. You will see a representation of your face, your skin, your bodily proportions, and so forth. You may note your height, and weight, and whether or not your hair is out of place. If you think about it, there is something very interesting about this process, because the acknowledgment and evaluation of your own appearance depends completely upon your knowledge of the appearance of other people. You have a sense of your height only as it relates to the evidence of height you've gathered from other people. Your judgment of your own weight depends entirely on your perception of the weight of others. Your idea of when you are having a good or a bad hair day depends on your attentiveness to current trends in fashion. In this way, key knowledge of yourself that is offered by a mirror depends upon our knowledge of others.

Now inasmuch as we can look at a physical mirror to see our outward appearance, where can we look to see a reflection of our inner person? Where will we look to perceive and evaluate our character? It is simple enough to grow in knowledge of our appearance—to see and remember our own skin—it is far more difficult to grow in the knowledge of the inner person. In this, there is no more challenging and effective way to grow in the knowledge of self than in committed relationship with your spouse. In marriage, you provide to one another a mirror that displays with stunning, piercing, and unsettling clarity the defects and deficiencies of your personal character. Furthermore, unlike your workplaces or friendships, the sheer closeness of marriage will expose—if not pronounce—those places that you hoped to hide. In this process, marriage divulges our wounds.

Where marriage touches on and exposes our woundedness, it is unwise and harmful to neglect the process of unpacking, or undressing, these wounds. And, let me be explicit, the revelation of wounds is going to be unavoidable—it is a component of leaving our families of origin and cleaving to our spouse. Therefore if you would grow in the knowledge of self, and if you would strive to be a tender recipient of the Lord's guiding hand into healing and maturity, then you must become adept at interpreting and responding to the images your partner reflects back to you. In this, understanding our anger will offer us a door through which we can examine our wounds. With wounds in sight we can strive for healing, and with healing we will gain new perspective on the whole of our life.

UNDERSTANDING GOD'S GIFT OF ANGER

Anger may seem a strange place from which to launch our discussion of self-understanding, but it is in fact a surprisingly appropriate one. Exploring our anger is a highly effective tool at unlocking self-awareness, and learning to acknowledge how anger tethers to other issues is critical in tracking our deeper wounds. To help us explore this, let's consider Paul's command regarding anger from Ephesians 4:26. There he writes, "BE ANGRY, AND YET DO NOT SIN. Do not let the sun go down on your anger." Within this short verse there are three clear sets of instructions—the first is to be angry, the second is not to sin in our anger, and the third is to deal with anger in a timely fashion.

The first of these commands may be the most surprising—and the surprise may lie in the fact that we are *commanded* to be angry. The Greek phrase Paul uses here employs the command form of the Greek verb. Anger, Paul tells us, is a right and proper response to certain circumstances, and we ought to feel it.

This may sound strange to you. You may have been taught, implicitly or explicitly, that anger is a forbidden emotion, that you ought not to show it, let alone feel it. And yet anger is in fact one of the emotions that God has given to us as a gift. Its purpose is to operate as a pain sensor for your emotional life. If you hold your hand over a candle flame, very quickly the small fire begins to scorch the cells of your skin. Those cells cry out to your central nervous system, and the cry is interpreted in your brain as *pain*. If your body is functioning properly, you will exclaim "ouch!" and retract your hand from the source of this pain. Pain, in this way, is an unmitigated good. It tells us when something is wrong, or when we are in bodily danger. If we lacked a sense of pain, we might hurt ourselves and be unaware, and to our horror our bodies would decay around us like the victims of Hansen's disease (leprosy).

In a similar way, anger is the sign that we are experiencing emotional pain. It is not itself the flame, but rather the signal to our heart that we are experiencing pain somewhere else. Anger notifies us that something is wrong, that something, somewhere, has happened that has hurt us. But unlike our bodies, for which the experience of pain is commonly localized to a very specific spot, the pain of anger requires discernment. The wound is not always obvious.

Thus, Paul commands us to "be angry." We ought to feel our anger. When anger comes, we ought to acknowledge and experience it. After all, it is telling us something important. However, because our bodies are marked and distorted by the effects of sin, our awareness of and responses to anger are not always right. When we become angry, therefore, we must ask some critical questions. First of these is this: Am I angry for godly reasons? This question marks the great dividing line through which we can discern the justification for our anger. It is possible that I have been personally wronged, or hurt, or neglected, and that my anger is a proper response to those circumstances. But it is also possible that I feel angry because I am responding to a perceived slight, or an imagined circumstance, or an exaggerated response. I can be justly angry in one circumstance (if in my workplace a coworker steals credit for my work), and unjustly angry with my spouse (when I take that anger and project it on him or her). When I become aware that I am angry, therefore, it is imperative for me to query my anger and ask, "Do I have a right to be angry about this?" One exercise you can attempt is to re-imagine the situation with the roles switched. If I had been the one to steal credit from my coworker, would he be just in his anger toward me? Such a perspective can help to jostle us out of our innately selfish and self-serving mindset.

Godly anger is a matter of being angry at the same kinds of things that anger God—things above all else that violate our human image in His likeness, things that demean the human creature, and things that prevent God's people from following Him. When Jesus strings together a whip in the temple courts, upsets tables, and throws out the money-lenders, he is angry because their presence in the temple has violated the purpose of the temple—they are buying and selling in the court of the Gentiles, where the nations are meant to gather and pray. In this way they have turned a "house of prayer for all nations" into a "den of thieves."[46] After the pattern of Jesus, we are creatures made in the image of God, designed to receive God's love and live in and through it. When people, circumstances, or our own ineptitude prevent us from fulfilling that nature, then anger is a just and godly response.

Once you've diagnosed the justification for your anger, there are two more questions to ask. The first is, "Do I need to forgive?" and the second is, "Do I need to confront to reconcile?" Not every experience of anger in your marriage will require a confrontation. Sometimes, in response to your anger, you will need to acknowledge the pain and then let it go. Your spouse has wronged you in some capacity—she has been late and made you late, he has been messy and you've had to fix it, she's said something incautious and it hurt, and so forth. You are justly angry at the circumstance, or the inconvenience, or the personal affront.

Regardless of the offense, you will be required to forgive, and the essence of forgiveness, remember, is the act of canceling your personal suit for damages.[47] You will let go of the wrong, completely. What you must discern is whether or not it is necessary to confront your partner in order to reconcile. For a large number of marital slights and missteps, simple forgiveness without confrontation is all that is required. But for certain circumstances, it will be necessary to speak about the issue. The purpose of such speech, let us be explicitly clear, is to make things right. You cannot begin in anger with the intention of making your partner share in your pain. The attitude of "I want you to hurt as much as you've hurt me" is not about letting go, but about laying the cost of your pain at your partner's feet. This is the antithesis of forgiveness, and is therefore more demonic than godly. Instead, Christian reconciliation begins with, "I need you to understand how this hurt me, so that we can make it right together." The goal is exposure, and not transference, of pain.

This brings us to the second and third of Paul's commands, that in our anger we ought not to sin, and not to let the sun go down on our anger. In some ways it is helpful to see these commands as outlining what we might call the masculine and feminine halves of anger. Men commonly respond to anger by flaring up and lashing out. "Do not sin" is therefore an appropriate rejoinder to men who occasionally fail to exhibit godly control over their emotional life. But this is still a command for both sexes to remember that we do not live at the mercy of our emotions. We *feel* a great many things, but none of those feelings may be used as a pretext for sin. And this is where a significant part of training in our inner lives and self-knowledge must occur. I must begin to disambiguate between the feelings I have and the responses I make to them. I must become a discerning feeler, choosing my responses to those emotions that present themselves to my awareness. In my anger, I must not sin.

The third command is what might be termed the more feminine side to anger, the command to deal with anger before the sun goes down. Contrary to many interpreters, we don't believe this means that you are required to deal with every argument before you sleep. Some arguments last too long, and are too important, to force through a night, and the process of forcing the argument might do more harm to your relationship than good. Instead, this command from Paul is an injunction to deal with all anger in a timely fashion. Don't wait to deal with it. Don't, in other words, stuff it. Many people (and, it seems, many women especially) bury their anger instead of processing it. Your partner does something one time, and rather than confront, you let it go. He leaves his socks all over the floor and you say to yourself, "He's busy," or "I'm sure he won't do it again." This goes on and on, but instead of forgiving, these little anger seeds get planted deep within where they grow and fester. Then, after the twentieth time, all of the anger comes out at once—sometimes explosively! In response, your spouse sheepishly picks up his socks from the floor and says, "It's just a sock." When we fail to deal with anger in a timely fashion, when we stuff and keep it within, it can come out in unexpected and hostile ways.

Now, while we've described these two kinds of anger as masculine and feminine, it ought to be clear that there are women who flare up, as well as men who stuff their feelings. The point is not to peg the genders one way or another, but simply to illustrate that anger is a gift that must be managed to be justly employed in our personal relationships. Refusal to explore and diagnose our anger will inhibit our capacity to grow in self-knowledge and godliness.

EXPLORING OUR WOUNDS

When it comes to self-knowledge, one door opens to another, and one room expands to a further one. When marriage presses us to process our own emotional responses it naturally tethers those emotions to wounds and pains that are more difficult to acknowledge. Some of these are pains we have spent our lives hiding, others may even be unacknowledged or unknown. In this, the necessary work of marriage offers an unprecedented opportunity to explore and receive healing for these deeper wounds.

This process began to come home to Jerry and Claudia after they had been married for about six years. For a period of about six months whenever an argument or disagreement would occur in their marriage, Jerry would overstate himself, absolutizing his position. This was characterized by statements like, "Claudia, you *always* do such and such" or, "Claudia, you *never* do so and so." Of course these overstatements were demonstrably false. Claudia, after all, is a complex person; she does not *always* do one thing or another. *Sometimes* she offers loving service to her family, *sometimes* she sleeps, *sometimes* she works, *sometimes* she communicates with friends, and *sometimes* she reads and studies. Such statements served only to aggravate and further inflame their argument.

Finally recognizing this process, Jerry would catch himself after the fact and apologize, vowing to himself to do better next time. Jerry is a slow learner (he wrote this). After about six months he caught himself in the very act of hyperbole (a serious crime indeed!). He said to Claudia, "You *always* . . ." and stopped mid-sentence to say, "No! That's not true!" then modified his charge by saying, "*Often* you . . ." He paused again, and tried another correction, "*Sometimes* you. . . ." At each modification Claudia gave him the most perplexed look, her facial expression capturing her confusion. It was at that point Jerry finally uttered, "You know, Claudia, you hardly ever do this at all; what's the matter with me that this bothers me so much?" Now they were getting somewhere. Through this process Jerry finally saw that the matter was actually a small one regarding Claudia, and the bigger issue related to why such a small thing bothered him so much. Why was it necessary for him to make such a big deal over something so relatively petty?

The answer lies in our goofiness. Goofiness is a way of describing our common, and characteristic, brokenness. We're all flawed, and we all bear wounds. We've had experiences, heard words, and seen things that have gotten Velcroed to us over time. We carry them around like baggage, and they manifest themselves by shaping and distorting our perceptions. Marriage provides us with a unique opportunity to identify, examine, grieve, forgive, and untether ourselves from these things. The original events can be quite small, and yet have disproportionate impact on the future. They can be simple impressions, picked up in childhood, what Owen Barfield described as a mere "whisper / which memory will warehouse as a shout."[48] To acknowledge our common goofiness, then, is simply to acknowledge that nobody has it together, and to do so in a kinder, gentler way. It grants that sometimes we hurt one another not because we are maliciously sinful, but simply because we're broken. We're goofy people.

However, as Jerry likes to say, there are two types of goofy people in the world: goofy people who *know* they're goofy, and goofy people who *don't* know they're goofy. This second group of people are dangerous, chiefly because they hurt other people but are unaware of it. They refuse to acknowledge that their baggage might shape their outlook, and rather than self-examine, they project their issues onto others. In this way, men and women who fail to acknowledge their goofiness become self-referential and utilitarian—unable to perceive how their own wounds shape their interactions with others, they are controlled by their baggage. They lay blame on other people for their own misbehaviors, and use people to get what they want. This is a problem in marriage because your spouse is guaranteed to activate your baggage. You will not be able to hide these things for long in the press of marriage. Genesis 2:24, speaking of the first marriage, says that the man will *leave* his father and mother and *cleave* to his wife. Surely this leaving and cleaving process also invites us to leave behind our wounds, and to discover in our cleaving a new healing, a new wholeness. Thus, the very closeness of your spouse grants you an opportunity to engage in the process of discovering and working through your wounds so that you can grow in self-awareness, becoming empathetic.

So, our anger flares up and we must begin the process of backtracking. Why am I angry? What is the source? It's normal to be angry when someone cuts us off on the highway, but if you're still angry after 20 minutes, tailgating and honking at the offender, then this ought to signal a deeper pain. It's normal to have spats and disagreements with your spouse, but when the anger becomes heightened or prolonged, we must pause and ask if our partner is really the source of our present emotions. Whether anger flares disproportionately, or whether it has become a generalized experience, there is a significant probability that you are actively projecting something deeper onto that particular incident. Growth in self-knowledge means learning to acknowledge the presence of our anger and following the tethers of our experience backwards to discover precisely what is tugging on them. It is in these moments that we must begin the deeper process of self-analysis. I may be angry with my spouse for saying a certain thing, but actually, I've come to realize that it wasn't that thing, but something else. Until we can get to the *something else* we won't really know what's motivating our heart. Until we can get to our *stuff*, we can't discover our wounds.

Our stuff, our baggage, is stuff we don't like to look at, but we've all got it. William Wordsworth wrote in his poem "My Heart Leaps Up" that "The child is the father of the man."[49] We are shaped by our childhood experiences, and they strongly influence how we perceive ourselves and our world as adults. What is more, very few people make it into adulthood unscathed by the wounds incurred during childhood. In our combined pastoral experience we've found that everyone seems to have between three and six really deep wounds—deep scars typically from childhood that have lasting emotional impact on today. These wounds behave like scratches on an old phonograph record. So long as a record lacked scratches, the needle would play the music flawlessly. But in the event that there was a deep scratch, the needle would jump and the record would play the same thing over and over, stuck at that one groove until you reset the needle. In much the same way, wounded people go through life normally until some experience reactivates their wound. Life can be going well in hundreds of areas, but one small comment can outweigh everything else and leave you reeling. Until the scratch is repaired, it can always be reactivated by the circumstances of life. Ralph Waldo Emerson, reflecting upon the untimely death of his son, wrote the following, "Sorrow makes us all children again, destroys all differences of intellect. The wisest knows nothing."[50] Present sorrows often tether our hearts to childhood wounds.

Encountering these scratches confronts us with our own incapacity to move on. Part of growing up and moving through life means that we develop ideal expectations about how things ought to be, about what kind of person we like to be. The trouble is that we all live beneath the level of our own expectations. We fail, and fall short, and other people fail us, and in the process additional things get attached to us. Our wounds bind us to the past, and our accumulated experiences become traps that inhibit intimacy. This initiates a process that psychologists call "repetition in search of mastery." We relive and revisit our old wounds, often unawares, in an attempt to find resolution. Sometimes this is what is happening when a couple finds they are arguing all the time. The real argument is not the one happening at the moment, but rather a kind of endless replay of old trauma. In this, we are attempting to work out our issues at the expense of our spouse.

But there are other ways that we manage our disappointment, and this is through the adoption of coping strategies. Since these deeper wounds are picked up in childhood and are often the consequences of issues within our families of origin, we are too young to deal effectively with these sorrows. A further complication is that none of us is particularly adept at self-healing. What commonly happens then is that we attach ourselves to surrogate experiences, coping strategies, that anesthetize our disappointments by assisting us to manage the emotional consequences of our wounds. These behaviors do not heal our wounds, but they deaden the pain and temporarily enable us to get by. These behaviors are often quite harmful.

Time passes and these anesthetizing behaviors become great liabilities warring against our proper development and maturity. Some of these behaviors are obvious, such as drug addiction, alcoholism, sexual addictions, and eating disorders. Others are more subtle, like workaholism, micromanagement, screen addiction, excessive video gaming, shopping, and serial relationships. In each case the anesthesia, while it helps us to cope with our pain, also deadens our capacity for intimacy with our spouse and children. Over time, the anesthetizing behavior begins to adopt the secrecy of the wound; we don't want anyone else to know that we're doing these things. Internet histories and credit card bills become objects that must be shielded at all costs. These behaviors become destructive to mature relationships. And one thing is also certain: you will be unable to hide your behavior from your spouse. The mirror will reveal all.

The apostle Paul in Romans 7 says that oftentimes the very thing we desire to do we don't do and the thing we find ourselves doing is something we don't want to do. Why do we keep going back to the things that we are ashamed of? Why do we return to these addictive behaviors that only deaden the pain but don't allow us to get better? It may be because our wounds are deeper than our convictions, and that we simply cannot get out of the rut on our own. We need help. And if we refuse to get help, we will become individuals who blame our spouse for our issues. Refusing the hard but honest look, we will hold the other person accountable for our wounds. Your life will be lived in reaction to the past, and your emotional life will be crippled and underdeveloped. Unresolved wounds such as these are also likely to be passed on to your own children, therefore dealing with these wounds is a necessary step in resolving the curse of generational sin.

When Jeremy was ten years old his parents separated and divorced. Children crave security and order, and the disruption in that family order occasioned by divorce is universally traumatic to children. One of the common responses is that children, feeling insecure, begin to try to control their environments, and this was Jeremy's experience. But the thing about control, when you are trying to control everything, is that you simply cannot, and failure generated deep and ongoing anger. Pornography entered early into this situation, and quickly became a powerful anesthetic to his disappointments. Control and anger began to shape his relationships with others, but lurking in the background was the ongoing reliance on pornography to make it through. By the time Jeremy married, he had the pornography aspect of his life in order, and yet there was still deep anger and frustration. It wasn't until he was in his first years in the pastorate that a few things happened. One was that he read the results of a long-term study of divorce.[51] Another was that he went through a six-month healing program called Journey Canada. It was then that some things really began to click for him. He realized how he had responded to his parents' divorce, and for the first time had an explanation of his own anger that made sense. Frequently, men view their struggle with pornography as the sole issue, and neglect to acknowledge that its origins are very often in the deeper wounds. To find healing in our issues with sexual sin, men must learn to examine their deeper wounds. In this process Jeremy was able for the first time to grieve that experience in some fresh ways and to see how his issues with control, sex, anger, and pornography were rooted in divorce. Understanding, and untethering, has brought healing.

Jerry's older brother Chester was sickly and had intense asthma and respiratory issues. Jerry remembers his mother steaming up the bathroom so that his brother could breathe at all, and his brother asking the question, "Am I gonna die?" Jerry loved his mother very much, but she had many of her own unresolved issues. One of them was that the stress of caring for a sickly child was too much for her. As a result, when Jerry had a cough as a child—about once every year—his mother would respond to Jerry by saying, "You just want attention!" She would then beat him for coughing. Consequently, when Jerry *did* have a cough, he would run to his room and try to hide it by coughing into a pillow. Jerry was also born without a sense of smell. Consequently, he never knew that his poop smelled, and as a child he would stay outside and play until he had messed his pants. His mother (not understanding the underlying issue) would rub his nose in his soiled underwear to punish him for it. The result was that Jerry grew up not only feeling deeply misunderstood, but anxious. He developed anxieties about life—he would compulsively clean, and sometimes certain sights and sounds would drive him a little crazy. Much later, after Jerry was married, he and Claudia had a difficult experience ministering to and then leaving a church. Claudia went to see a therapist, and wanted Jerry to go as well. Jerry agreed to go for Claudia's sake, figuring that he had no issues to deal with. But in the counselor's office Jerry's stuff all started to come out, and with the stuff came weeping. He later brought his sister to a session, and she recounted his childhood stories from her perspective, adding things that Jerry himself had forgotten. The process brought deep healing to places that were unexpected in Jerry's life.

These wounds, and our compensating behaviors, and how we experience the presence of God all appear to be linked. Jim Houston, founding president of Regent College, likes to ask people three different questions: What is your earliest relational wound? What is your compensating behavior? How are you experiencing the presence of God?[52] Jeremy's earliest relational wound is his parents' divorce, his compensating behavior is control, and how he experiences the presence of God most powerfully is in worship—in the *loss* of control in God's presence. Jerry's earliest relational wound is feeling unloved by his mom, his compensating behavior is anxiety and fear, and he experiences the presence of God most powerfully in evangelism—in bringing people to know the unconditional love of God. In this way, the healing of these wounds has opened our hearts to fresh areas of service for God.

HEALING AND THE THREE ROOMS

One further story can help us to see how these wounds find healing. In many years of ministry, this is one of the saddest stories we've encountered. There was a boy whose mother died when he was four or five years old, giving birth to his younger brother—an early, and deeply traumatic wound. His sorrows were compounded by the fact that he was raised in an extremely abusive family, and as often happens in such families he was picked on more than anyone else. When he was about seventeen years old he was kicked out of the family and forced to find his own way in life. He was able to find work and worked quite hard—in fact, his work ethic won him a series of rapid promotions. But just when things were looking good, someone else at work filed a sexual harassment suit against him. For the record, we are convinced that the charges were false. Nevertheless, because of this false accusation he was sent to prison for seven years.

Here is a man with many scratches on his record. Is it possible for him to find healing? The answer, of course, is yes. In fact, his story is well-known—his name is Joseph. Joseph's mother, Rachel, died while giving birth to his brother Benjamin, and his other brothers were abusive to him. They abused him because they envied both their father's favoritism and Joseph's natural capacities. Interestingly, this story reveals generational issues as well. You would imagine that Joseph's father, Jacob, after his experience of favoritism from his own father and his brother Esau, would do better with his own sons. Joseph's brothers sell him into slavery, and it is while in service to an Egyptian nobleman named Potiphar that Joseph flees Potipher's wife's sexual advances. She levies her charge against him and Joseph is imprisoned for seven years.

Many years later, when Joseph is elevated to the position of second-highest official in the land, he takes an Egyptian wife and with her has two children. The names of his two children reveal something of Joseph's healing process—of leaving behind his old wounds and cleaving to a new life through his marriage. The first boy is named Manasseh, and translated the name means "I forget." Joseph claims in Genesis 41:51 that "God has made me forget all my trouble and all my father's household." The Lord had made it possible for him to let go of the negative experiences that marked his childhood. The second son's name is Ephraim, which means "Fruitful," and of this child Joseph says in Genesis 41:52, "God has made me fruitful in the land of my affliction." Healing, for Joseph, involved leaving behind his old pain and embracing a new fruitfulness.

For us, our process of healing is likely to involve a journey through three different rooms—the Good Will Hunting Room, the Dark Room, and the Wounded Healer Room. In the film *Good Will Hunting*[53] Matt Damon plays the title character, a brilliant but deeply wounded young man. He works as a janitor at MIT, but has the mind to solve the most complex math problems presented to him. However, a traumatic childhood involving abuse and foster care prevents him from intimacy and joy. He ends up in the office of a therapist played by Robin Williams, who quickly realizes that Will Hunting is using his vast intellect as a shield against pain. Their sessions progress, and they develop a relationship. In the critical scene of the film Robin Williams presents Matt Damon with his file, which includes the police records of his beatings and foster-home history. They share battle stories of beatings for a while, but then Robin Williams turns with sudden intensity and says to Matt Damon, "It's not your fault." Damon shrugs it off, but Williams won't be deterred. "It's not your fault," he repeats, again and again. Damon becomes more and more visibly upset, trying to move the conversation on. But in this moment, the therapist is able to break through the exterior, and for the first time, weeping, Will Hunting realizes that he isn't responsible for the sadness in his past.

This is the Good Will Hunting room. It is the place where we realize that we've experienced and inherited the baggage of others, that other people's goofiness has damaged and wounded us. It is where we realize it is not our fault when our parents divorce, not our fault when our mothers cannot express their love to us properly, not our fault when we are betrayed by the generational sin of our parents. In this room, our realizations have power to lance the cyst, and press out the accumulated pus from our hearts. And if the image seems grotesque, it is appropriately so—these things are ugly and must be unbandaged and aired in order to heal. We realize that we are not our stuff; we differentiate, and in a fresh way we get to source our identity in Christ.

As a result of time spent in the Good Will Hunting Room, we must practice forgiveness. Forgiveness bears deep resemblance to grieving, and must be processed emotionally. No one walks away from the funeral of a loved one and concludes that "It's over. I no longer need to visit this emotionally." The grieving process demands that tears will often visit us until the grieving process is complete, and this may take years. Similarly, forgiveness requires that one processes, over time, the emotional trauma of past pain. We are grieving over those events where the record of our life was scratched.

This will require time and labor, and we will find, to paraphrase an observation by C. S. Lewis, that everyone thinks forgiveness is a marvelous idea until he has someone to forgive.[54] Imagine having a couple of hours on your hands, a long drive, or a day retreat. If you sit in silence and there is unresolved pain in your life, it will often come bubbling up to the surface of your conscious mind. Your first impulse will likely be to shut this out, whether by turning on the radio, or browsing the Internet, in order to anesthetize with distraction so that we don't have to enter into the dark memories of past pain. We have to choose to fight this impulse and allow the emotion to come to the surface. In this, you will get angry all over again, and sad all over again, and grieve all over again. But with time and in prayer you will be able to bring these memories to a place of forgiveness. Perhaps it will take a few hours, or even a day, to get to that place. Later, these memories will come again, and perhaps as we grow in maturity we will be able to find that place of forgiveness more quickly—maybe even only five minutes faster. In this way, forgiving, and forgiving again, seventy times seven times, we can begin to repair with forgiveness this deep scratch on our hearts. In time, the memory and the forgiveness can come almost simultaneously, and in such a moment a Manasseh has been born into your life as well. In this kind of refined forgetfulness, God is helping you to forget the pain of the past through the repeated application of forgiveness.

But healing doesn't stop there. From the Good Will Hunting room we must travel onward to the Dark Room. In this room, we come to the dark realization of those things that *are* our fault. We recognize the truism that hurt people hurt people. In Luke 6:40 Jesus reminds us that the pupil, "after he has been fully trained, will be like his teacher." We have been taught by broken people, and we pick up by contagion both the virtues and vices of our teachers. We have imitated their brokenness. In the Dark Room we are exposed to the irradiating light of God's truth— our memories show one picture, but in negative we are enabled to see the shadow side of our lives. We are made accountable for our own sin.

As a result of time spent in the Dark Room we must seek forgiveness from the people we have harmed. To the best of our ability, we must seek to make things right with the people we have wronged in our own brokenness. These acts of seeking forgiveness must be very specific. We must recall, and seek forgiveness, in those places where we are aware of having acted in brokenness. Asking for forgiveness means that we cannot make excuses. The word "but" cannot enter in. "I am sorry about this but I was X. . . ." This is not asking for forgiveness. All the same, we bear in mind the realization that we were doing the best we knew how.

The final room of our healing is the Wounded Healer Room. In this room, the light of our personal illumination helps us to see others differently. It is here that empathy bears fruit. I must reason that if I have done things that were a product of my brokenness, and if I have committed acts that require forgiveness as well, then perhaps the person who hurt me is also wounded. Thus, from our own wounds we are enabled to see others with fresh and loving eyes. Receiving the surgery to remove the log from our own eyes, we see with tender clarity the specks in other people's eyes. Perhaps we can remember Job, who, after he has met with God, must offer sacrifice for his three friends. Part of Job's healing, in other words, is found in ministry to others. In a similar way, Jeremy's healing is found through leading people to commit more of their lives to God, and Jerry's through bringing people to faith. Our wounds, then, in healing become special avenues for ministry.

There are a multiplicity of wounds, and there are many paths to healing. The good news is that you don't really have to wait for marital conflict to begin exploring them. You can begin by examining where it is that you experience the presence of God most powerfully. What does that tell you about your inner life and expectations? You can also examine emotions other than anger. The next time you watch a movie or read a novel and experience sadness—the next time mist begins to form in your eyes and you work to hide it—take a moment and examine. Pause the film and debrief the experience with your spouse. It might just be a doorway into new self-understanding.

Can we expect to find healing for each of these wounds? In a sense, yes. As we grow in relationship, in empathy, and in self-knowledge, we become aware of how we've been hurt and how we live out of those hurts. Wounds, of course, are tangled messes, crisscrossing and making a mess of our life's circuitry. But as we trace one string through the mess, it can give us fresh clarity regarding the others. And healing in this way also gives us hope. If, given time, Jerry and Jeremy were able to discover God's healing in particular wounds, does it not suggest that, given eternity with God, all other wounds will be healed? We may never fully untangle the mess in our lives, but this process enables us to grow in hope.

SELF-KNOWLEDGE AND THE JOHARI WINDOW

In 1955 Joseph Luft and Harrington Ingham put their heads, and their names, together to create the Johari Window, a simple metric that helps people to understand some of the complexities involved in self-knowledge. It is especially relevant as it touches on the issues of communication in marriage. The Johari window contains four panes, dividing our self-knowledge according to what we know and don't know, and what the world knows and doesn't know. Each pane reveals a feature of how we perceive ourselves and are perceived by others.[55]

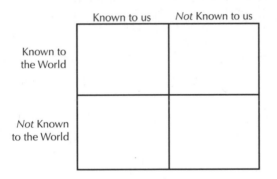

The first pane, in the top left, reports things that are known to both us and the world. This is open, public, and obvious information, such as whether you are blonde, brunette, red-headed, or bald, whether you are Asian, Indian, African, or Caucasian. People generally discover quickly if you are gregarious or reserved, whether you are mechanically inclined or challenged, whether you are artistically talented, or literarily inclined, or if you gravitate toward math and sciences. These are things that you know about yourself, and others know about these things too. The first pane contains few mysteries.

In your relationship, this first pane is the place of first attraction. You see a boy or a girl across the room and your heart starts to race. After all, at this point you can know little of his or her inner life, and the first blush of attraction is typically grounded (innocently enough) in this category of superficial knowledge. What you learn about one another on a first date typically covers this information as well. Where do you work? What are your hobbies? What kind of family do you come from?

The second pane, in the top right, reports information that is known by the world but *not* by you. These are your blind spots. Imagine if you left home in the morning with a booger hanging from your nose. If throughout the day you never looked at a mirror, this would be something obvious about you to the world of which you yourself are blissfully unaware. The same would be true of a zipper down, or makeup misapplied, or hair out of place, or toilet paper attached to your shoe. If, at the end of the day, you finally look into the mirror and discover your appearance, you are likely to be mortified. If only someone had shared the information with you!

In marriage, the things we don't know can hurt us. What is more, if we fail to make known certain things to our spouse, those things can also hurt us! Here, in the second pane, is where our spouse offers feedback on our life. This is the wife telling the husband that he cannot wear plaid with stripes. It is the husband telling the wife that, indeed, that dress does make her look heavier than she is (be careful!). In fact, when it comes to matters of our personal appearance we are often eager to hear the information our spouse has to return to us. But what about those situations when the information relates to character or an annoying personal habit? "You were unkind to that person just now." "You're late and making us late as a family again." "Do you realize that when you tell stories at parties you often make yourself look good?" These are aspects of our lives about which we require the mirrored perspective of our spouse to address, but how often are we willing to hear that critical voice? While we are eager to fix the smudge on our face or to address a misplaced zipper, we are often less receptive to the criticism that addresses a bad habit or poor character trait. There must be a place in marriage to lodge complaints without triggering arguments, and it is here that our skills from communication, covered at length in the previous chapter, must be put to practice. Learn to trust the information your spouse supplies, and hold these conversations in a spirit of love and concern, not of control or manipulation. One thing that will help is to select good timing (not right before bed, perhaps!), and to be gentle. Gentleness is helped by beginning with what is called a "soft startup"— in other words, talk about something good before you get to the complaint! Better yet, individuals within marriage can be proactive and can actively request criticism. Would you help me to see my blind spots? In this way, the second pane of the Johari window provides insight into one of the most powerful channels for personal growth.

The third pane of the Johari Window, in the bottom left, reports on things that are known to us, but unknown to the world. These contain, among other things, our secrets, our fears, our quiet ambitions, our family histories, our joys, bitterness, sadnesses, expectations, and some of our wounds. Most of our lives are lived from this pane, and this is the area of life that we choose to share in intimacy with our spouse and select friends. To know someone, and to be truly known, requires us to be vulnerable at this level of self-knowledge.

In your relationship, you must choose to share these things. Very often, your capacity for intimacy will itself be shaped by your willingness to divulge your inner life to your spouse, and good marriages cultivate the kind of trust whereby self-disclosure is a significant part of the relationship. Additionally, remember that self-disclosure breeds more self-disclosure. As we practice this habit in love and consideration, we will find the process increasingly less threatening and more enjoyable. But beyond this, many of these things are what will be revealed and exposed in the iron-sharpening-iron process of leaving and cleaving, as you discover who you really are in the presence of your spouse. Because of this, we must acknowledge that these stories and secrets are precious treasures, and must be treated as such by each partner. If a husband shares his deepest childhood wound with his wife, and later she tells a friend about that wound, this will damage your intimacy. If a wife shares a damaging experience with her husband and he laughs at her, this will inhibit intimacy. In almost no circumstances ought you ever to share these kinds of things with a person who is not your spouse, and above all with a person of the same gender as your spouse! This pane contains the currency of intimacy, and if you as a husband or wife spend it with another woman or man then you are sowing the seeds of adultery.

The fourth pane of the Johari Window, in the bottom right, reports information that is unknown to both us and the world. These are characteristics buried deep inside of us, characteristics that only life circumstances are likely to squeeze out of us. Soldiers engaged in a landing assault on some foreign beach, hearing bullets pinging against the steel landing craft, fully knowing that in moments the front of the craft will open up and they will have to charge into a volley of bullets, have no idea *how* they will act until the moment comes. Then, it will be revealed what they are made of. A woman, wired with all of the potential for mothering and nurturing, can never actually know what kind of a mother she will be until she has children of her own. A man or woman who have had a lifelong curiosity about sex, wondering what kinds of lovers they will prove to be, have no idea of actually knowing until they are married and the opportunity is properly placed before them.

In your relationship, it is in this fourth pane that we are confronted with both uncertainties and hopes; here we come to the limits of our own experience. In this pane you and your spouse will navigate all the unknowns of your life and future together. Here we require grace, and prayer, and understanding. Here, hand-in-hand, you are given an opportunity to walk in grace and deep self-discovery. To know and be known for who you really are—to become fully human in the presence of another person.

Toni Dolfo-Smith, executive director of Journey Canada, grew up in South Africa as a Christian struggling with same-sex attraction. In adulthood, he made the decision to live as a fully homosexual man. He was in a committed same-sex relationship, and involved with a church that sanctioned his relationship, but he felt dissatisfaction in his life. A process of healing brought him to an awareness of his deeper wounds and a conviction that God was calling him out of a homosexual lifestyle. Today, Toni is married with children, and people occasionally ask him when he felt that he was healed of his same-sex desires. Toni's answer to this question is terribly important—because he doesn't claim to be healed from the desires. Instead, he draws two pictures.

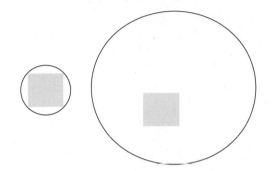

In the picture on the left, the square represents Toni's sexuality, and the circle his personhood. When he lived in the homosexual lifestyle, his whole personhood was defined by his sexuality. There wasn't very much of Toni *apart* from his sexuality. But in Christ, Toni has experienced an expansion of his personhood. The result is not that his same-sex desires have gone away, but rather that they have been newly framed by his life in Christ. They may still be part of his life, but they are not the whole of his life. In the same way, our wounds can dominate our whole outlook on life. But as we grow in empathy and personhood, they are given new perspective—put in their place, if you will. The result is that we are enabled to live differently in light of our wounds.

This chapter has covered a huge amount of information, and we ought to keep a few things in mind here at the end. First, we must remember that failure to engage in the process of exploring our wounds will invite projection. Closing our vision to the mirror of self-reflection invites us to blame our spouse, our children, and others for our problems. But safely traversing these dangers also demands a more perfect love. We ought to remember John's words from 1 John 4:18, that "perfect love casts out fear." Perfect love, love that is secured and immovably grounded in God's love, destroys our fear. This suggests that imperfect love creates anxiety. Fear is produced in our hearts because we distrust love, and in divulging your life to another person—from what you know, to what you don't know—you must strive to advance in a spirit of love. The more your love is perfected in Christ's love, the more fearless and abundant will your marriage become. In time, growing in wholeness, empathy will mature, and this new wholeness will create opportunities for healing for others—self-knowledge giving birth to self-knowledge, intimacy begetting intimacy, and love, ultimately, begetting greater love.

ASSIGNMENT

Spend some time as a couple with the Johari window. Go back and forth and share information about one another based on each of the four panes. What is something you learned that you didn't know before?

Journaling is an indispensable habit in the process of growing in your self-knowledge. If some of the features of this chapter have seemed obscure, commit twenty minutes each week to quiet reflection and journaling your experiences. Follow emotions, and arguments, and feelings as you've encountered them throughout the week. Over time, reflect back on those experiences and attempt to draw some conclusions. What can you learn about yourself from this kind of longer view?

Have you ever shared the earliest relational wound you can remember? What is it, and how do you think it has shaped your life?

PART 3

Exploring Expectations

Chapter 9
Exploring the Expectations of Family and Culture

Chapter 10
Exploring the Expectations of Parenthood

Chapter 11
Exploring Financial Expectations

Exploring the Expectations of Family and Culture

Let's call the whole thing off.
—George and Ira Gershwin

ON THE CLASH OF CULTURES

Jerry and Claudia once lived in England during a sabbatical leave. While there, their children would ask questions about why the English did things the way they did. Jerry and Claudia explained that, for whatever the particular issue was, it was something proper to English culture and that the American custom was, in that environment, unusual. Then they asked their children to watch carefully and see if they could figure out *why* the English did things that way. It wasn't long before their children gained a fair understanding of British motivations. This, however, led to a fresh inquiry—"Why do we do things the way that *we* do them?" Again, Jerry and Claudia challenged their kids to see if they could figure it out, and once again they were able to come up with some compelling and well-considered reasons. This, in turn, led to a further inquiry, "Which way is right?" Explaining that sometimes there aren't necessarily right or wrong ways to do things, their children realized a freedom to deliberately choose for themselves. Consequently, they adopted some English ways of doing things, and became more deliberately American in other ways. Their short time in another country made it possible for them to gain fresh insight into their own culture.

Pastoral Theologian David Augsburger writes that "Anyone who knows only one culture knows no culture."[56] Like the fish unaware of water, monocultural individuals lack awareness of the air they breathe, the environment they inhabit, and many of the assumptions that govern their lives. Rudyard Kipling in his poem *The English Flag* asked the following question, "[W]hat should they know of England who only England knows?"[57] Who indeed truly knows their home who hasn't visited other homes and learned firsthand what makes his or her home unique and special? In this, the only real way to learn your culture is to be brought to its boundary. As Augsburger writes again, this is because "culture becomes visible on the boundary, in comparison, in contrast."[58] It is when we are brought to the boundaries of our experience that we learn that others think, behave, and draw conclusions in ways vastly different from our own.

Jeremy and Liesel lived in British Columbia for over ten years, an experience that made them aware of Canadian culture and offered fresh insight into their own American identity. They were startled to discover that pedestrians will walk into the street anywhere and expect traffic to stop for them (a procedure that, in other cities, would result in increased traffic deaths!). They were puzzled to find that common grocery items such as chocolate, ketchup, and Coke contained more sugar (there are ten calories more in a Canadian can of Coke than in an American one). And they also quickly became alerted to what might be called Canada's "Little Brother Syndrome"—the perception that Canadians feel they are always warring to identify themselves *against* big brother America to the south. Looking to themselves, however, Jeremy and Liesel were awakened to the extent of America's isolationism. In 2005 President George W. Bush signed into law a bill that altered the start date of Daylight Savings Time. At the time, there was some frustration in Canada because a change in time zones is one that affects the continent, not simply a nation. It illustrated that Americans regularly make decisions without reference to the rest of the world. Another element they came to recognize was the unique overlap of religion and politics in America—one that is not in existence in Canada, and one that causes Canadians no small amount of confusion. The point, overall, is that life in a new country helped Jeremy and Liesel to see both Canada and America with new eyes. Culture is a thing that only becomes visible on the boundaries.

MARRIAGE IS A CROSS-CULTURAL EXPERIENCE

Inasmuch as this is true for geopolitics, it is also true in marriages, because every marriage is itself a cross-cultural experience. Unless you are marrying your sibling (which is illegal), each member of a new partnership brings a set of assumptions about the world and the way it ought to operate that are shaped by their alternate childhood home lives. We bring to our relationships foods, habits, customs, and protocols that are attuned to our specific preferences, and may be fundamentally different from those of our spouse! In the famous George and Ira Gershwin song, a couple laments these differences precisely—one says either (pronouncing it ee-ther), the other says ay-ther; one likes potatoes, the other potahtoes. Faced with these difficulties, the singer concludes, "Let's call the whole thing off!" Some of these differences can certainly seem insurmountable!

Jeremy, in marrying Liesel, married a *Texan*, and this was significant. It meant that he would be introduced to more barbecue (delicious), as well as Texas t-shirts, Texas-shaped pasta, and waffle makers that produced Texas-shaped waffles. It also meant, more seriously, that there were certain expectations regarding conflict in public. Namely, that it ought *never* to happen in public. Liesel came from a family that never argued at all, while Jeremy came from a family that valued heated debate. Naturally this generated some conflict when it came to resolving difficulties! The truth of the matter is that every family has its unspoken rules and cultural norms. As children we are socialized to know, understand, and properly respond to these norms, and yet the process that indoctrinated us to these norms may or may not have been directly articulated. This, again, is why it is only on the boundary space between our cultures that we become aware of the embedded protocols of our own family culture.

The best insight into your own family's rules and protocols—into the culture of your family of origin—is your spouse. Unfortunately, these quiet rules become visible and pronounced the moment your spouse *breaks* such a rule. Perhaps you've got an uncle with one leg, and while you know the story, you also know that nobody is supposed to bring up Uncle Jimmy's missing leg. Everyone in the room goes about their business pretending that there's nothing going on. Then, one day, your wife-to-be meets Uncle Jimmy and asks him, innocently enough, but to your growing horror, "What happened to your leg?" She didn't know the rule. During Jeremy's first Christmas at Liesel's family home, he was puzzled to find that nobody spoke at the dinner table. He struggled throughout dinner and after to keep a conversation going, but it was an uphill battle. After the meal, the husband of one of Liesel's cousins (someone who had married into the family) approached him and thanked Jeremy for talking at dinner, saying, "Nobody talks in this family!" In these matters, it is a good rule of thumb to monitor the "shoulds" you feel in your partner's presence. When you feel a strong sense that she *should* behave a certain way, or that he *shouldn't* have done a certain thing, then this is a strong indicator that you are making a judgment from some of your unspoken family expectations.

Blending families can feel like playing a game where nobody articulates the rules, and without a good sense of humor about these things couples can certainly struggle. It will help, first of all, if couples can view these revelations above all else as opportunities. There's an old story about a wife who, preparing a pot roast for supper, cut off the ends of the roast before putting it in the pot. Her husband, looking on, asked why she did that. "That's the way," she explained, "that my mom always did it." They phoned her mom and asked about this technique, and her response was to say that she'd learned it from *her* mom. Finally calling grandma, they asked once again, hoping to learn the true secret of the family pot roast recipe. Grandma answered, "I always cut the ends off because my pot was too small!"

In marriage, you are being offered a chance to consider, and to evaluate, the unexamined architecture of your thought life. Some of the things you discover will be good, others will be bad. Either way, the goal is to make a studied and reflective choice about each one with your spouse. After all, it is together that you are choosing the kind of home you want to have for yourselves and, ultimately, for your children. The passage from Genesis 2:24 is once again illuminating—the man shall *leave* father and mother and *cleave* to his wife. In marriage two individuals are leaving their culture of origin and together creating a new subculture, one that is a blend of both. The process of blending will require a degree of awareness, analysis, and pruning: certain familiar things will necessarily be lost to both partners. However, the new family, created by you and your spouse, will be a uniquely new thing, unknown and not yet seen in the world. It will be a unique reflection of the one-flesh nature of your marriage.

For relationships where each partner is of a different ethnicity the rules remain the same—*every* marriage is a cross-cultural experience, and each couple is therefore required to evaluate their assumptions regardless of their ethnicity. Still, marriages that bridge ethnic barriers can bring some special challenges. There may be a need for increased empathy and impartiality—how your spouse views the world may be strikingly different from how you view it. One factor, complicating matters, is that we often feel that "culture" can be used as a label to excuse activity. This activity or behavior, in other words, cannot be changed *because* it's culture. To take this line is to sidestep the critical work of evaluation, and the truth of the matter is that culture is not valueless, and we are not valueless entities within culture. Culture remains answerable to absolute standards of right and wrong. Jeremy has heard, in his office, a man explain that it was okay to beat his wife because his own dad had beaten his mom. "It's part of our culture," he claimed. We had to clarify that culture cannot be used as a label to sanction abuse. In India for many years it has been a custom for men, when they have spent their wife's dowry, to drive the woman to suicide or burn her alive. That way, the man could remarry and claim another dowry. While this practice might be culturally acceptable, it also has another name: evil. These are extreme examples, but it is critical to remember that culture itself is one of the things that is evaluated in marriage.

Another thing to keep in mind is the role that language plays in a mixed-ethnicity marriage. When one member of the partnership has access to a language that the other does not, this can create possibilities for exclusion. In other words, it is possible to communicate contempt of your partner at the level of language itself—so be careful! Additionally, it can be tempting at family gatherings for one spouse to speak to his or her parents, or for the parents to speak to one another, about the outsider spouse without his or her knowledge—to complain, or offer snide comments, or other unhelpful judgments. To be inhospitable in this way is deeply unhelpful. In the event that this happens, the spouse who can translate *ought* to do so—and in this way dispel the veil of secrecy.

In the end, this blending of families is a creative activity that can bond a couple with increasing intimacy. It is something you are creating *together*. So work to keep culture something fresh—a surprise to be uncovered rather than a bugbear to be avoided. Remember Chesterton's words that the world will only starve "for want of wonder." In this, the magic of the other can, and should, be magnified by culture.

HAPPINESS, PEACE, AND FAMILY PROTOCOLS

It will help to understand these protocols if we imagine for a moment that each family gives its children a kind of road map to happiness.[59] Your parents, through their direct instruction, through the example of their own marriage, through the stories they told, through their punishments and encouragements, planted into you a vision of how the world ought to look. Within that world, they guided you to a set of behaviors that, if you follow the rules, you expect will generate the maximum of happiness. If the map has a city on it called "Happiness," then perhaps our family of origin has taught us that the road to happiness leads through a town called People Pleasing—the best way to make it in life is to upset no one. Or maybe the journey goes through Economic Accumulation—happiness is found when you are financially sound. The journey can go through Education—happiness comes with the best grades and the highest degree. Other towns can include places such as Hard Work, Honoring the Family, Never Getting Angry, Success, Fame, and so forth.

These protocols can be both positive and negative. The positive protocols can build a solid foundation for your life, giving you a sense of identity, strength, stability, and trust from your family. A person socialized to wholesome values from their family of origin can typically travel far down the road of success. However, the negative protocols can cripple you, tearing you down, creating anxiety, fear of failure, uncertainty, and low self-esteem. A person socialized to negative values may struggle especially with intimacy and happiness in life. Additionally, these protocols can be communicated both implicitly and explicitly. We gather implicit data from how dad treated mom, how mom related to a brother or sister, how dad treated work, how the family handled success, failure, or tragedy. We gather explicit data from the stories our parents tell about what is valuable in life, from their direct encouragements and discouragements.

Jeremy is half Puerto Rican and half American, and on his American side he remembers growing up hearing stories about his grandfather. A child of the Great Depression, Wallace Duckworth fought in WWII in the Army Corps of Engineers. After returning home, he and his wife moved with their infant daughter from Oklahoma to Southern Illinois with nothing but a car and $25. He took a job laying electrical line, then in the oil fields, then purchased a service station. He would work at the service station seven days a week, making enough money to purchase a house, then another house (both bought with cash!), and eventually purchased nearly a whole city block of property in their small town as well as a car wash. The message, taught to Jeremy *explicitly* about his family of origin, was that Hard Work was the path to happiness.

On his Puerto Rican side, Jeremy's father grew up in extreme poverty in Puerto Rico. His grandfather, Herminio Rios, also fought in WWII, but was a career soldier and remained in the army after the war. On one occasion he and his unit of Spanish-speaking soldiers were under attack, and Sergeant Rios, because he could speak English, was sent to pass on a message. While he was delivering it, many of his men died. Later, stationed at Ft. Sill in Oklahoma, he would study for more education while training young officers on the firing range. After his military service, he retired into pastoral ministry. The message of his life, quite *implicitly*, was that Education was a path to success. As a result, of Jeremy's aunts and uncles, two are nurses, one is a teacher, and one is a pastor with a Doctor of Ministry degree. His dad is a lawyer. Whenever Jeremy graduated from anything in life, he came to expect cards from all of his Puerto Rican family congratulating him on his degree. Again, the message was passed on quite clearly, if implicitly: Education is the path to happiness.

As a result of these two influences, it is not surprising that today Jeremy is both working toward his third degree, and struggling with overwork! Knowing these protocols, however, helps him to make choices about both how to live his life in the present, as well as what kinds of messages he wants to pass on to his own children.

In addition to family stories, these protocols are often passed on in more subtle ways. From our families of origin, we typically inherit little sound bites that replay in our minds, often without our conscious effort. Some of these, again, are implicit, like a "whisper / which memory will warehouse as a shout" (Owen Barfield). Others were directly spoken in our childhood homes. Fredrick Buechner says that the three laws of a dysfunctional family are "Don't trust, don't talk, don't feel."[60] Other common phrases are things such as "Only family can be trusted"—the belief that things ought to be kept in house as much as possible. "Don't make dad angry" is a belief socialized by discipline and fear. "Women are not equal" is a message learned in many homes from how dad treated mom. "Boys don't cry" has been taught explicitly to many young men, crippling their emotional development. One of the common phrases that Jeremy has encountered working in Asian churches is the belief, communicated directly and indirectly to young Asian women by their moms, that "If you're not beautiful enough you'll never get a husband." Many young Asian women live with significant anxiety because this sound bite runs through their minds.

Such beliefs are deeply ingrained in us—indeed, many of them are subconscious. This means that when our spouse begins to break the rules of our family of origin, or operate his or her life according to a map for happiness that points to different towns on the journey to happiness, this can generate significant conflict. After all, our spouse is not merely breaking a rule, but he or she is violating our beliefs about what it means to be happy! It's almost as if he or she was doing it on purpose! When we encounter these difficulties, it is important to keep in mind that our instinct will be to retreat to what is comfortable. In other words, difficulties in marriage can drive us to withdraw to the comfortable structures of our families of origin, whether good or bad. The wise couple must commit to turning *toward* one another when they encounter these difficulties. In this you've got to cultivate, as much as possible, the habit of having a conversation about your expectations. Take time to discuss how each of your families of origin managed these circumstances, then try to consider if there might be more than one way to resolve the conflict. If you find you have reached an impassible frustration together, then seek the counsel of a trusted friend, pastor, or professional counselor. The individual should be able, from his own unique perspective, to referee your discussion and bring clarity. If, even at that point, you personally cannot reconcile yourself to the solution, then it may be necessary for you to visit a counselor on your own to work out how the rules of your family of origin have so bound you that you find it difficult to accept the viewpoint of another.

Each person brings a unique perspective to marriage and is affected, whether for good or ill—by our backgrounds. We all bring excess baggage to our marriage. Seeking help to navigate these issues is not a sign of weakness—sometimes they are as difficult to see and perceive as the air we breathe. Overall, however, in a healthy relationship the variety of cultural backgrounds relative to ethnicity, economics, education, geographical preferences, food, language, preferences, and so forth, should be *celebrated*. These are simply the unique strands of your individual lives that are being patiently twined into the tapestry of your unique life together.

NAVIGATING COMMON FAMILY ISSUES

There are quite a few common family issues that a wise couple can discuss together beforehand. For example, it is good to have a discussion about holidays. Where do you spend Christmas? If both sets of in-laws live in the same town, do you visit one home on Christmas Eve, and the other on Christmas Day? Do you switch it year by year? What happens when you have your own children? Do you have Christmas at your home and invite both sets of parents to join you? What are the protocols for when the whole family is together? Are there special expectations for weddings, funerals, or anniversaries? If your spouse's family are of a different religion, what impact does that have on your expectations? If a Buddhist grandmother passes away, are you expected to bow before her grave? These kinds of discussion are best to have *before* the event happens.

What about children? You need to remember that your children are, in fact, *your* children—not your parents' children. When grandma and grandpa go home, you are the one who hangs on to the child, and it is you, ultimately, who is responsible for how the child turns out. In some Asian cultures there are strong cultural pressures to eat, behave, and dress certain ways while pregnant and as a new mom. One Korean custom is that the mother, after the birth of her child, is not supposed to bathe for over a month. If you've been enculturated to these customs have you taken the time to evaluate them? What choices will you and your spouse make about how to raise your children?

What about gifts? If your spouse's family gives you a gift as a couple, what strings are attached? If your father-in-law offers to place a down payment on a house for you and your bride, what are the consequences of this gift? Later, will it become *"our* house"? Will they expect to move in with you? Questions like this are not meant to make you refuse generosity, or to encourage you to be suspicious or ungrateful, but to ensure that both parties are aware of what's at stake in a given transaction.

What about names? What are you supposed to call your new in-laws? Mom and Dad? Mr. and Mrs.? Do you call them by their given names? Discuss it together and make sure you clear it with your in-laws as well!

What about conflict? What do we do when there is difficulty between the couple and their in-laws? One solid principle to observe is simply this: for any conflict with in-laws it is the child's job to defend his or her spouse, and it is the spouse's job to love. If the husband's mother is making things difficult for his wife, the wife must simply love. The husband must be the one to speak up for his spouse. After your wedding day you are one flesh—you have left mother and father and are joined to your partner. Therefore if your parents complain about your spouse it's a bad idea to agree with them—even if you agree with them!

Consider other points of exploration. What about rest and restoration? Did one family recover by going out to eat? Did another by retreating to your rooms? Was shopping a therapeutic exercise? What role did books play in your family? Are you aware of your own energy preferences? It is a common misconception that extroversion and introversion are measures of a person's capacity for social interaction. Instead, these two metrics indicate an individual's preference in how energy is restored. Some find that energy returns most in solitude, while others are restored by being in groups. How did your families respond to your preferences? Failure to understand our energy preferences can create a situation where one partner retreats (to recover) while the other chases, which makes the first partner retreat further, which makes the other partner chase more. Without some comprehension of your energy preferences this can become a deeply frustrating trap for both of you.

Remember, with each of these categories you are in the business of creating a new family together, a new culture, one that will, to a degree, trump the former culture. It is important, when you chose to go against the established system (which you have already done by marrying someone outside the family), that you are aware of what you're doing. Have the discussion, attempt to view both sides with impartiality, then make a decision about how you respond *together*. Too many individuals behave reactively toward their families of origin—their lives are lived in reaction to the past, rather than in reflective action with relation to the past. This creates vows—a promise made to the self to *not* be like our parents. Because this vow is made reactively, it typically goes too far—committing the opposite error that we are trying to avoid. A child who grows up in a high-conflict family may vow never to argue; and yet there are some things worth arguing about and fighting for!

In the end, your job as a couple is to act toward the world as a united front. Act, behave, choose, and think of yourselves *as one*, because that is what, in marriage, you are.

ASSIGNMENT

Take some time to discuss the "Common Family Issues" from the last few pages. How did you do things in your childhood home? How were they done in the other partner's home? Make the effort to ask why such things were done. If your parents are still living, phone them up and ask them.

Proactively ask your partner what his or her perception of your family of origin is. Remember that he or she is offering a first impression. Work together to get to the heart of what makes you, and your family, tick.

Recommended Reading: Boundaries, by Henry Cloud and John Townsend (Grand Rapids, MI: Zondervan, 1992).

CHAPTER 10

Exploring the Expectations of Parenthood

Mrs. Goldstein was walking down the street with her two grandchildren. A friend stopped to ask her how old they were. She replied, "The doctor is five and the lawyer is seven."
—Thomas Cathcart and Daniel Klein

The whole child stands before you as a little creature of God, on whom He desires to work through you.
—Evelyn Underhill

NO JOB DESCRIPTION FOR PARENTING

In 2009, Liesel gave birth to the Rios's first child, a boy they named Moses. Coming home from the hospital was a strange experience. The nurses, who had so intently focused on Liesel during delivery and in the hours following, insisted that a proper car seat was essential for dismissal from the hospital. Arriving with the seat, and securing their new precious cargo in it, they permitted them to leave. But this was the terminus of their care. They gave no instructions in how to provide or care for this new little creature. There was no manual of operations that arrived with Moses's life. There was no question of our suitability as parents, or our capacities—moral, mental, or physical—to support a life. This is an astonishing experience.

Of all the tasks we are commissioned to perform in life, parenting is the single greatest one for which we are given precisely no training at all. Where do we learn? Many of us simply attempt to draw from our own experiences as children. Of course, none of us remembers what it was like to be a baby, so this is a limited resource. Others have had experience with younger siblings, but where do the younger siblings learn? Furthermore, repeating the parenting of our families of origin often simply recreates our own brokenness.

Where else do we learn how to be parents? From television families? But these are geared for absurdity—situations orchestrated to accent irony and stupidity. (Note that in such families the fathers are often comic buffoons.) Do we learn from books? Have you visited the parenting section of a bookstore lately? Shelves upon shelves of books with contradictory information. What about psychologists? But do we even agree with them about what it means to be human? What about doctors and nurses? An older friend of ours had three children—with the first, the nurses insisted that the baby absolutely *must* sleep on its belly. With the second child (several years later) the nurses insisted that the child sleep on its side—it was the *only* way. With the final child (again several years later), the nurses insisted that the child sleep on its back—anything else would *kill* the baby. Which way is it? The sea of contradictory information creates an overwhelming set of standards and encourages reactivity rather than reflection.

What, you will ask, about the Bible? Doesn't the Bible give us instruction in how to raise our children? The answer is that things aren't as clear in the Bible as we might like. Most of the parenting relationships in the Bible are fractured—by favoritism, abandonment, infighting, and a host of other issues. It reminds us of what Thomas Fuller, a seventeenth-century English pastor, wrote during his study of the genealogy of Jesus in Matthew 1.

> Lord, I find the genealogy of my Savior strangely checkered with four remarkable changes in four immediate generations.
> 1. Rehoboam begat Abia; that is a bad father begat a bad son.
> 2. Abia begat Asa; that is a bad father a good son.
> 3. Asa begat Jehoshaphat; that is a good father a good son.
> 4. Jehoshaphat begat Joram; that is a good father a bad son.
> I see, Lord, from hence, that my father's piety cannot be handed

on; that is bad news for me. But I see also that actual impiety is not always hereditary; that is good news for my son.[61]

Put frankly, the Bible simply doesn't operate like a manual for parenting; rather, we must extrapolate from the Scriptures what it means to be human in God's image and then train little, tyrannical, wild creatures to think, feel, and act in godly ways. It is an overwhelming task.

In this process we get one big help, and walk with one enormous liability. The help is that God is revealed in the Scriptures to be our Father. In other words, we get to look to Him and draw from Him a model for how to parent our own children. In this, we see that there are no perfect fathers in the Bible *but* God. The liability is the fact that while God is perfect, we are not. And none of us can possibly compare to Him as parents.

What we'll do then is attempt to outline three principles for biblical parenting. It would be impossible to outline everything that could possibly be said about parenting, but hopefully these three principles will enable you and your spouse to have an enriching discussion about how you plan to parent your children together.

PRINCIPLE 1: PARENTAL LOVE MUST BE UNCONDITIONAL

Paul says in Romans 5:8, "But God demonstrates His own love toward us, in that while we were yet sinners, Christ died for us." The love of God is revealed to us in an *unconditional* way. It does not depend upon our quality, our effort, our performance, or our innate goodness. Quite the opposite, it was most powerfully demonstrated on our behalf when we were living in abject rebellion toward God. By extension, when we are communicating love to our children—and children learn love and the meaning of love most clearly from their parents—we have a Christian mandate to love them unconditionally. There are three further ways that we can ensure our love is right.

First, we must never use love as a tool for discipline. Many children grew up in homes where their parents would give and withhold affection as a means of getting the child to behave. Food, gifts, attention, and physical touch were offered on the basis of performance. More explicitly, some parents would say things like, "I would love you more if you behaved." Or, one parent would vocalize love for a behaving sibling and neglect to mention the misbehaving one—an omission that rings loud. The lesson learned by children in such homes was that love is conditioned by our performance. Such children will grow up learning both that they are fundamentally unworthy of love, or that they must earn love from everyone in their lives.

Second, along with this, you must remember that you have permission to dislike your children. Loving them unconditionally does not mean that you must like them all the time or necessarily approve of all their actions and choices. There will be times when your children actively disappoint, frustrate, and even enrage you. In practice, this is an extension of something you already do with your own body— you continue to love yourself in a fundamental way, even when you occasionally dislike yourself for overeating, or for oversleeping, or for messing up a relationship or event. In the end, your commitment to loving your children unconditionally recognizes the need to discipline them occasionally.

Third, it is important to remember that you are not really your children's friends. In Evelyn Underhill's words, "The whole child stands before you as a little creature of God, on whom He desires to work through you."[62] God is performing a work to raise up the child under your care, and you will in many ways never fully graduate from this responsibility. You have been given a sacred authority by God, and in the image of your creator God, to see that your children are raised in the knowledge of the Lord—to maturity, character, and faith. While there are parts of your life that will, in time, come to approximate friendship as your children grow older, there will remain a level of your authority that will never quite pass away. Buddy parents are bad disciplinarians; in prioritizing friendship they have lost sight of the purpose of the parenting. In turn, their children lose sight of the meaning of having a parent.

1 John 4:18 says that "There is no fear in love; but perfect love casts out fear, because fear involves punishment, and the one who fears is not perfected in love." The perfect love of God makes fear flee from our lives—but if this true, then the corollary might also be true, that imperfect love creates anxiety. The person who doesn't know that he or she is loved by God will constantly seek to find love and affirmation from other people. The individual will live in a state of anxiety, never certain of the love of people, distrusting of intimacy and closeness, seeking the approval of others to feel secure. In the end, if you want your children to stay out of trouble with drugs, alcohol, and sexually inappropriate behaviors, then one of the best things you can do is ensure that they are secure in your love.

The Grant Study was a landmark project that followed 268 Harvard graduates over a period of 75 years and determined, overwhelmingly, that the single most important factor in wealth, happiness, and stability later in life was warm childhood relationships.[63] The Scriptures, similarly, tell us that we are beings *made* for love, in the image of a God whose nature is itself *love*. To deny love to our children violates something in their created nature. It is, perhaps, the worst violence of all that you can do as a parent to your child.

PRINCIPLE 2: DISCIPLINE MUST BE GIVEN WITH REFERENCE TO PURPOSE

Proverbs 22:6 famously instructs Christians that we ought to "Train up a child in the way he should go, even when he is old he will not depart from it." This is good advice—so long as we have some concept of what is meant by "the way he should go." Without that—a clear understanding of purpose—then your discipline will go astray.

We should clarify that this sense of purpose is *not* your personal selection of career for your children. The opening quotation of this chapter is a joke about one Jewish woman asking another the ages of her grandchildren—her reply: "The doctor is five and the lawyer is seven."[64] It is all too easy to be projective—to demand that our children fulfill careers *we* have chosen for them, for our own ends, ideas of self, and social status. But this is simply an imposition of our will upon our children, an effort to live by proxy through their lives.

Instead, the goal of Christian parenting—the purpose for which we are called to discipline—is to raise our children to be mature, Christian adults, to operate in the fullness of the image of God. We are tasked to train them in moral reasoning, good decisions, discernment, the use of freedom, responsible action, and godliness. Discipline is the tool we use to guide them toward this purpose.

Hebrews 12:4–11 speaks about the way that God the Father disciplines us, and from that passage we can draw some understanding of our own discipline.

> You have not yet resisted to the point of shedding blood in your striving against sin; and you have forgotten the exhortation which is addressed to you as sons,
>
> "MY SON, DO NOT REGARD LIGHTLY THE DISCIPLINE OF THE LORD,
> NOR FAINT WHEN YOU ARE REPROVED BY HIM;
> FOR THOSE WHOM THE LORD LOVES HE DISCIPLINES,
> AND HE SCOURGES EVERY SON WHOM HE RECEIVES."
>
> It is for discipline that you endure; God deals with you as with sons; for what son is there whom his father does not discipline? But if you are without discipline, of which all have become partakers, then you are illegitimate children and not sons. Furthermore, we had earthly fathers to discipline us, and we respected them; shall we not much rather be subject to the Father of spirits, and live? For they disciplined us for a short time as seemed best to them, but He disciplines us for our good, so that we may share His holiness. All discipline for the moment seems not to be joyful, but sorrowful; yet to those who have been trained by it, afterwards it yields the peaceful fruit of righteousness.

It is the nature of discipline to be unpleasant, and yet its purpose ought to serve for our good. In this, we see two different aspects of discipline. The first is that discipline is simply a tool for training. Like a workout at a gym, a diet, a schedule, or a personal regimen, the discomfort of implementing the discipline is married to the reward of a fitter body, better weight control, management of our time, or management of our affairs.

Jerry used to come home from trips and bring small penny candies—like a mint or a butterscotch—for his kids. The kids came to expect the treats. One day Jerry changed the conditions. He told them, "You can have the candy now, or you can wait until tomorrow and I'll buy you a ten-dollar toy at Toys"R"Us." At first, the kids took the candy, but eventually Jerry's son Jeremy wised up and chose to wait. It was hard for him to watch his siblings eat their candy, but on the next day when Jeremy came home with the ten-dollar toy they felt differently. This is a discipline that is not grounded in punishment, but in the training of our children's moral reasoning—especially as it applies to principles of delayed gratification!

But in addition to training, discipline as parents also covers punishment. Proverbs 13:24 offers the following warning: "He who withholds his rod hates his son, but he who loves him disciplines him diligently." Neglecting to discipline has the potential to destroy your child. On another occasion Jerry left his kids, who lacked self-control, with a bowl of unopened Hershey's Kisses and instructions not to eat them. He returned later to find the evidence of chocolate kisses smeared all over the faces of his children. As parents of young children we might take pictures of such a moment and remember it with humor. However, such an act of intemperance, while funny with a child, loses its mirth when as a young adult he or she is sleeping with his girlfriend or her boyfriend. Punishment in such a situation might seem irrelevant at the time, but the lesson learned has much farther-reaching ramifications.

It is important to pause for a moment and speak with extra caution. We recognize that not every family will agree on the means that parents will use to discipline their children. In this, we intend to speak very carefully, and to move from areas we believe should be generally agreed upon, to areas where we might disagree.

First, whenever you discipline you must discipline to the level of comprehension of the child. In this, discipline is never a one-size-fits-all business, but requires attentiveness and creativity. Yelling at your infant is meaningless. Lecturing your five-year-old on the cost of replacing your damaged carpet is an exercise in futility. Telling your teenager that he cannot have any candy after dinner may not have the effect you desire. In this way, and in all acts of discipline, the "rod" must be specially attuned to the comprehension of the child.

Second, it is critical to discipline according to the needs of the child. Again, discipline is not a one-sized-fits-all business—the needs of your child will change from month to month, and from child to child. In this, you have access to a wide-ranging toolkit of disciplinary options. Do you raise your voice? Threaten? Remove privilege? Give a time out? Ground? Apply a physical punishment? The key factor is to *learn* your child, then marry the right punishment to the child. When you apply the punishment, make sure that it's fair, and work to make sure it reaches the mark. As the child grows in maturity, the needs for discipline will naturally shift.

Liesel and Jeremy have three young children who regularly bathe together. One day they were banging on the bath doors and Liesel warned them to stop or they would be taken out of the bath. Standing outside the door, and out of sight, Liesel heard their daughter, Cates, say, "Let's bang on the door and blame it on Asa" (the youngest). Moments later, there was a bang, and Liesel walked back inside, where the two older kids proceeded to frame their younger brother! Removing them from the bath, Liesel came to consult Jeremy. How would they discipline in this situation? They needed their kids to learn that framing their brother, then deceiving their parents, were serious offenses. Coming on a moment of inspiration, Liesel remembered that Cates had just received a new stuffed animal and was terribly excited to bring it to church and show her friends the next day. For his part, Moses had just received a quantity of Pokémon cars that *he* was excited to share with friends at church. They decided that punishment would be that both kids would have to leave home their respective toys. This may sound innocent enough, but the results were fantastic. *Both* children were reduced to wailing and tears, deeply saddened that their actions would prevent them from engaging in their joys. Meanwhile, Liesel and Jeremy were laughing so hard they had to turn their backs on the kids!

Discipline like this doesn't always work—and Liesel and Jeremy will be the first to tell you that they don't always get it right—but *that* time it worked, and it was glorious because they were able to reach the heart, and that is the essence of disciplining according to the needs of your child.

Third, it is critical as parents that we discipline dispassionately. Children are guaranteed to generate anger in your life. We should be clear that there are real times for discipline to be marked by anger—if your child is running into the street and about to be struck by an oncoming car, we expect that your discipline *ought* to be tinged with a little anger! But for the most part, all discipline should be considered and applied studiously. If the child commits an act worthy of discipline, as much as possible insert a pause. Send the child to his or her room first. Take time to calm down, breathe, and gather your thoughts. Then select the discipline that is most appropriate for the situation. This process is important because it enables us to choose our discipline rather than react to our children. Additionally, if you are angry you are liable to discipline more forcefully than you would otherwise. A commitment to being dispassionate will prevent you from overstepping yourself in discipline.

Now, to offer comment on the question of physical (corporal) punishments. First, parents must discuss the question together and agree. If both of you don't agree, then you mustn't use physical punishments for disciplining your children. Talk about your families of origin, what worked, what didn't work, what you liked and didn't like. Have an honest discussion about the role of discipline in your family home.

We have found physical punishment to be an important tool in our parenting toolkit. One of the principles of the world, it seems evident, is that where you will not be taught by reason or reward you will be taught by pain. This is simply a principle of how the world operates, and in parenting we are instructing our children in these rules. However, once again it is critical that these punishments be administrated with reference to purpose, according to the needs of the child, and dispassionately. Arbitrary physical punishments will create anxiety and fear in the child. Excessive physical punishments (striking the face or legs, use of a belt or spoon) are abusive and often do long-term damage. It is critical, therefore, when you are planning to discipline physically, to take the time to reaffirm the love of your child both before and after you've administered the discipline. Take time to explain the reason for the discipline, and attempt to explain it to the understanding of the child. Make sure that you communicate the extent of the punishment clearly. Then administrate, and hold the child until his or her heart is repaired. Although you are disciplining, you want to ensure that your relationship has been prioritized throughout the process.

As children mature, the metrics of discipline will naturally change. From punishment and reward, discipline will likely become a matter of increasing freedom and responsibility. Bedtimes, curfews, use of a car, phone, computer, and so forth, these freedoms must be offered proportionately. As the child shows the capacity to manage these freedoms well, he or she will warrant the trust of more freedoms. If he or she shows mismanagement of freedom, then this necessitates the loss of privilege. This, perhaps more than any other place, is where you don't get to be your children's friends, and indeed for a time might be their worst enemy. But *not* going to a party, or *not* keeping their phone, or *not* having access to a computer in their room might be exactly what is warranted by their maturity at that given time.

PRINCIPLE 3: PARENTS ARE SINNERS

Romans 3:23 tells us, "for all have sinned and fall short of the glory of God." The "all" there includes parents as well, and parents will do well to remember that they are, indeed, sinners. While we are called to be like our heavenly Father in love and in discipline, yet we remain sinners and fall short of His perfection. We love imperfectly, discipline improperly, hold double standards, project our own issues onto our children, work out our own anxieties through them, and we recreate the damaged parenting structures of our own childhoods. In this, we are all sinners and must repent.

The passage from Jeremiah 31:29–30 is illuminating. The proverb in ancient Israel had been that "the fathers have eaten sour grapes and the children's teeth have been set on edge." But Jeremiah promises, speaking for the Lord, that no longer will this be the case, but each person will suffer for his own sin. We are not bound to a law of generational sin, but given power and access to live differently. The process, however, will require self-awareness, as well as confession of sin.

This is not a general confession of sin that you must perform, but a specific one. When you have overstepped yourself as a parent, you must apologize to your child. When you have overstepped yourself with one child, you might well need to apologize to the others as well. Failure to do this can cause our other children to become collateral damage. If you have been unkind to your spouse in the presence of your child, that also will warrant an apology. If you have imported frustrations from your office life into your home life, that will require an apology. If you have neglected your household duties, then that will require an apology. You will be required to apologize more than you would like.

Ephesians 6:4 commands parents, saying, "Fathers, do not provoke your children to anger, but bring them up in the discipline and instruction of the Lord." The word translated "provoke" there can also mean exasperate, or enrage. Parents will exasperate their children when they discipline arbitrarily or without reference to purpose. We exasperate our children when we fail to live to the standard to which we ourselves claim to follow. In this, we exasperate them when we fail to ask for forgiveness when our sins are self-evident to them. They conclude not that we are perfect, but that we are hypocrites.

Your children, perhaps more than anyone else in your life, will see your sin. This is inevitable. What is not inevitable, but which you must do, is they also must see you humble yourself and ask for forgiveness when you have done wrong. This will not always be easy. It may feel at times like losing your parental authority and edge. And yet it is the only way to ensure that your children learn that your Christian faith is serious with everyone in your life.

In all this, Jesus's words of Luke 6:40 resound prominently: "A pupil is not above his teacher; but everyone, after he has been fully trained, will be like his teacher." A fully trained child will be like *you*, and yet the most important aspect of our parenting is that we seek to raise our children to know Jesus. This suggests that if you, as a Christian, are unformed—or malformed—then your children are also likely to become unformed or malformed in their faith. Asking forgiveness will be the simplest, most everyday, and one of the most effective ways to model this sincere faith in your family.

ASSIGNMENT

Set aside time to discuss parenting in your family of origin. What do you think your parents got right? What do you think they got wrong? Can you recall a time when you feel that you were disciplined unfairly? What about a time when you were disciplined fairly?

CHAPTER 11

Exploring Financial Expectations

Under three things the earth quakes,
And under four, it cannot bear up:
Under a slave when he becomes king,
And a fool when he is satisfied with food,
Under an unloved woman when she gets a husband,
And a maidservant when she supplants her mistress.
—Proverbs 30:21–23

THE ECONOMICS OF A MARGIN

*W*hen you were young and learning to write for the first time, chances are your teacher provided you with a piece of manila-colored writing paper with pale blue lines on the paper. The lines were alternately solid and dotted, solid and dotted. The dotted lines were designed to help beginning writers to learn how to distinguish capital letters from lowercase ones. Carefully, if you were practicing your letter "n," you would trace your pencil up to the dotted line, then back down to the solid one. An unpracticed hand, however, would blow past the guideline and attempt to correct its way back down. In learning to write, you were required to learn what it meant to draw within the margin of the paper. In a similar way it is necessary for young couples preparing for marriage to learn the art of living financially on a margin.

It is unfortunate that many couples live their lives from paycheck to paycheck, barely keeping financially afloat. In fact, statistics reveal most people live beyond their means—writing, as it were, their financial lives outside the margins of their means. Couples that live at ground zero are likely to dip up and down beneath the line. At times they will be flush with funds, but other times they will find themselves in the red. In such a state, living hand to mouth, when a financial crisis occurs they are in big trouble—an unexpected pregnancy, a car accident, a home repair, a surprise bill, a health crisis. These challenges can quickly deplete your financial resources and drive a couple so deeply into the red that they are left wondering if recovery is actually possible. A result will be that the couple's economic life is lived solely attempting to reach zero again. The unexpected crises that are simply part of life will come in time to make the couple feel as if they are swimming against a strong current, never able to recover.

The English word "economics" derives from the Greek word for house, *oikos*. It covers the business of effectively managing household affairs. The business of managing your family finances has the potential to be the most contentious aspect of your relationship. Disagreements about the purpose and utilization of money plague many couples with frustration. While financial success does not and cannot map onto marital happiness, stable financial structures do encourage your relationship and preserve it from unnecessary stress. To break the cycle of ups and downs, living at the mercy of whatever emergency comes next, a couple can make a conscious choice to live on a margin—that is, they can deliberately build a buffer zone between ground zero and where they are living their economic lives. To do this, you must choose to communicate about your financial expectations and to keep one another accountable. Although economic wobble is inevitable, such a couple would find strength, control, and even a measure of intimacy in managing their common financial life.

DISCUSS THE VALUE AND PURPOSE OF MONEY

The place to begin with your family finances is to have a candid discussion about the meaning and purpose of money in your family of origin. Perhaps you came from a family in poverty and resources were tight as a child. Perhaps your family was hit by tragedy after tragedy and never really recovered. Perhaps you had a parent who spent uncontrollably and racked up credit card debt that became a burden to the rest of the family. Perhaps your parents were both accountants and kept track of every penny spent by every member of the household. Perhaps a parent had a gambling issue. Tendencies to hoard or spend freely are both sourced in these perceptions of money formed by our childhood. Whatever the story may have been, money in your family of origin *meant* something, and you as a couple must work to discover what that something is, whether it be pleasure, or security, or power, or a tool. It is unlikely that you and your spouse will automatically agree on the deeper value of money.

A discussion like this can help to sort out many common issues between couples. If one partner views money as a tool for pleasure, then he will be more likely to want to use it to take a trip overseas. But if the wife views finances as security, that trip overseas might be seen as a threat to the family's future. Our responses to one another's spending, in this way, is shaped by our expectations as to the value of money. The discussion of finances will tie directly into your discussion of family of origin.

In addition to money's value, a couple should have a discussion about the meaning of wealth. What are your financial goals in life? What number in the bank answers for the needs of the future and for your shared ideas of success? Additionally, couples should discuss the difference between the *appearance* and the *actuality* of wealth. You aren't likely to be able to have everything, so what luxuries are important to you both? And what sacrifices are you willing to make for the sake of greater goals?

The wise couple will also discuss the difference between investment and consumer debt. Investment debt is for things like the purchase of a house or a loan for tuition. These are *investments* that will bring a return. Consumer debt is when you go into debt for the sake of a consumable—such as furniture, a new car, or an expensive family vacation. Investment debt ought to be reasonably considered and thoughtfully undertaken; consumer debt ought to be avoided. In line with this, make sure you talk about the role of credit cards. If one of you has a problem with credit card debt, it would be best to get that in the open now, and to ensure that that partner is given limited access to credit in the future! As a rule, you should never purchase something with a credit card that you cannot pay off in the next month.

You should also discover which of you is a better manager of personal finances and elect to put that person in charge of the family finances and keep the books. Schedule regular conversations to discuss your financial position and overall goals, and remember that good management is not the same thing as control (i.e., whoever is managing finances is not there to control the other partner's spending). It's also a good idea to agree with one another how much is permissible to spend *before* you consult your spouse. One friend of Jeremy's left his home one Saturday morning with one car and, to his wife's astonishment, came home with a different car! At what threshold does it become necessary to ask your husband or wife before you write a check, click "purchase," or swipe your credit card?

Have a discussion about how you will manage your banking. Are you both banking at the same location? Which bank is better? Are your checks automatically deposited? Some couples like to maintain separate bank accounts, but we think it is better to have a joint account. After all, you are entering into one life, and separate accounts can signal a hold-out of territory and distrust between a couple. Either way, commit to open books with one another. If you are concerned about your ability to purchase gifts for your spouse, then arrange for regular cash personal allowances that can then be allocated for surprise gifts.

In the following sections we are going to give some general advice on the allocation of funds. Such advice will be necessarily general, but we trust that the principles will be clear enough to lodge within your imagination and there to bear fruit. They fall into four groups—three groups of 10%, and one of 70%.

GIVING—THE FIRST 10 PERCENT

Proverbs 30:21–23 describes four things that trouble the earth, and one of them is "a slave when he becomes king." Money is a slave, a servant of other ends. Ungoverned, and unexamined, money has the potential to become king, and as a king money is tyrannical, ruining the lives of you and your spouse. In its proper place, money has the power to serve your family. Giving is one of the most powerful ways to ensure that money remains a slave, and not a king.

In this, the Bible is exceptionally clear that believers are to culti-vate generosity. In the Old Testament, this takes the form of a custom called tithing, which is the dedication of the first ten percent of your resources to the work of God in the world. This tithe would provide for the needs of the Levites, Israel's priestly class, as well as maintain the temple infrastructure. Symbolically, it points to the fact that *all* of our resources belong to God. In giving the first ten percent, we are sancti-fying the whole. In view of this, we want to suggest that the first step toward developing a financial margin in marriage is to give ten percent of your income away.

To some people this may seem silly. Jerry occasionally taught premarital courses where non-Christians were present. He well remembers one couple that informed him that they felt no obligation to give because they weren't Christians. Jerry told them that he understood what they were saying, but added that God didn't command tithing because He needed the money. This suggests that the principle, if true, must have a more universal application. It suggests, perhaps, that people of means are in danger of developing hoarding self-interests relative to their money. If a marriage is designed to have love at its center, then habits of charity will serve to enhance this love and contribute to a more fulfilling life overall. In the end, no one who is serious about a healthy marriage can neglect the cultivation of charity.

Giving—generosity—is mandated for God's people, but the manner of giving remains unspecified. A couple ought to be aware of the needs of their local church and invest appropriately in that organization. In this, it is certainly possible that some people may choose to simply give a portion of their paycheck each week or month. But it is also possible for couples to diversify their giving. In this, find a cause or a charity for which you are both passionate (or pick one each) and commit to giving in support to that group. Are you passionate about children? Then give to a children's charity such as Compassion International. Do you have a burden for the suffering church? Then consider giving to the Voice of the Martyrs. Do you have a passion for economic development? World Vision might be the place to look. Your commitment to setting apart 10 percent of your income for God's use can be as intellectually engaging as any other pursuit in your common life together.[65]

Conceivably, a couple could also choose to invest their yearly giving into a trust fund. Each year, then, they could invest 10 percent into the trust, and commit to giving a portion of that money away. While in the first years such tithing would appear skimpy, over time they might discover that they can give far more away and to far more significant causes. Imagine that a couple earns 100,000 dollars their first year of marriage and they put 10,000 dollars into the trust. At this point, all of the money in the trust is given away—they legally cannot touch it for personal use. The money can now only be used for the purposes prescribed by the trust. At the end of the year a percentage of the trust, say 4 percent, is given away, reducing the total slightly. The following year, if the couple's income increases to 110,000, then the tithe input into the trust is 11,000 dollars. In this way, the trust can grow over years, and in time the couple can give away far more than their original 10 percent. Actual giving to support God's work in the world will be substantive.

Giving, in these ways, is an important part of your intellectual intimacy, and can become a means of instructing your children in what it means to be charitable and generous. When you invite your children to the table of your family finances, you can give them a vote in what charities the family will support in a given year. Imagine what it would be like for your children to become the kind of people on the lookout for other people's needs, eager to find ways to match needy persons with resources. Cultivating such generosity bears fruit far beyond the simple act of giving.

RETIREMENT—THE SECOND 10 PERCENT

Many young couples think that retirement is a long way off—and it is! But it is important for couples to make plans now for their future years. In this, it is far better to be prepared than surprised. Many companies offer matching programs for retirement funds—they take a portion of your paycheck each month and match it with money. It is unwise *not* to take advantage of such an offer. Regardless, if you can, take the next 10 percent of your income and commit it to your retirement fund. Remember that little bits go a long way over time. Consider that $5 per day for 20 years is about $36,500. Such simple accumulation can make a huge difference in your life after retirement. Additionally, couples ought to consider life insurance as part of this portion. This will ensure less financial stress in the event of an untimely death.

In this area—of your financial future and investing—couples would do well to acquire a basic education in finance. We recommend that a couple, shortly after marriage, set up a series of appointments with financial advisors. Meet with quite a few—as many as between eight and ten. Set a common agenda where you inquire about what kinds of financial programs they offer and what they believe your situation requires. At the end of the meeting, chances are the planner will want you to sign the paperwork on the spot. Inform him or her that you are planning to meet with several other people first. If the agent tries to pressure you, then don't give him your business. If, after finding out that you are planning to meet other people, he offers you a plan that *wasn't* on the table before, then mark in your memory that this may indicate that he or she is not as trustworthy as you might have thought. With each agent you meet, and with each presentation you hear, you will become more and more savvy regarding annuities, retirement funds, insurance policies, and so forth. You will ask questions that will probe more intelligently into the inner workings of this important, and helpful, business. The eight to ten weeks of meeting with these various agents will prove to be something like a tuition-free college course in personal finance, and, at the end of the day, the two of you will be able to discuss among you as to whose product looks best and which agent seemed the most reliable and likable. The decision will be made corporately and you will enjoy clarity concerning your future.

SAVING GENERALLY—THE THIRD 10 PERCENT

Life happens, and there are things you will need to purchase, vacations you would like to take, and household and family needs that will require resources. In preparation for these events, you ought to save. Take 10 percent of your income and lay it aside in a dedicated savings account, and this will provide a healthy buffer between you and economic ground zero.

Within your savings, as a couple you will benefit if you commit to withholding on all major purchases until you have the cash in hand for that purchase. In this, you are encouraged to build a habit of acquisition that falls clearly within your margin. This will prevent you from needing to go into the red to make necessary purchases—let alone luxury purchases. If you need a piece of furniture, or are planning a trip, or will require a new car, then plan and begin to save. (Note that new car purchases are almost always bad financial sense—the car loses immense value the moment you leave the lot.) Save more than 10 percent if you know the purchase is forthcoming. The chief exception, of course, would be the purchase of a home.

It is important for your own hearts that you train yourselves in delayed gratification, especially because the delays can bring about surprising changes. Many times in Jerry and Claudia's marriage they sensed a desire to buy something and began saving accordingly. Once, when their children were small, they thought it would be nice to buy a piano so the kids could take lessons. They saved and prayed that God would lead them to something affordable that would meet their needs. When they had saved up to five hundred dollars (no small sum at that time!) a couple from their church told them that their parents were moving into a retirement home, they had a piano, and wanted to know if they would have a use for such a thing. Jerry and Claudia gladly accepted the gift and kept the money they'd saved in their savings account, beefing up their margin a bit more. This kind of thing has happened with some degree of frequency over the years, and it has been fun to watch as they have saved and prayed.

If you've had your discussion together about the difference between the appearance and actuality of wealth, then those principles will help you to make decisions about what kinds of things ought to be purchased immediately, and which kinds of things can wait.

DEVELOPING A BUDGET—THE REMAINING 70 PERCENT

With the remaining 70 percent of your funds establish a budget. Most families, if they have two incomes, will be able quite reasonably to live on 70 percent of their joint income. In this, you must remember that a budget is a financial goal and not a moral standard. Falling short of a moral standard should make you feel guilty because you are looking up to see how far you've failed. Falling short of a goal ought not to make you feel guilty because your view is more reflective—look how far I've come! A budget, then, is a goal that helps us to stay on a trajectory of financial responsibility.

Budgets are approximations; they are not always exact, and the approximation that will become your budget must be developed through experience. Take the 70 percent number of your joint income and, over the next three to six months, track your primary expenses. This will give you time to account for the variety of fluctuations that affect every financial plan—from annual changes in climate that alter your electric and gas bills, to insurance renewals, or summer trips. The six-month view will enable you to average your bills and these averages can become the framework for your budget. In this way, your budget is inductive—reflecting reality, not fantasy.

As a rule, a good budget will make allowance for housing, utilities, food, transportation, car payments, gas, oil changes, maintenance (setting aside money for tire replacements, overhauls, etc.), parking fees, tolls, clothing, entertaining, hospitality, entertainment, home improvements, gardening, painting, repairs, health care, personal allowances, and so forth. Whatever the realities of your actual spending—realities discovered during the three to six months of monitoring your financial output—these become the categories for your budget.

One final budget category will be your buffer. This is a measure of cash-on-hand, separate from savings, retirement, and giving, which can provide a buffer against zero in your monthly budget. Say, for the first months of marriage, that a couple is able to set aside $1000 as a buffer. This becomes the new "zero" of your bank account. Then, if one of you needs dental work and it requires a $500 withdrawal, make an effort to rebuild that buffer—but add another $100 to it this time. In this way, you can build your buffer to such a degree that your habits of family acquisition fall within your buffer and never require you to draw from any other pot to make it work. Perhaps you will need to forgo entertainment or personal allowances for a few months to make up the difference, but the end result will be a greater sense of personal control and security in matters relative to your family finances.

Finances don't have to be a domain of struggle and contest between couples, but can be a life-giving and enriching expression of your joint life together. Living on a margin can be a great way to get started on that journey.

ASSIGNMENT

Read Proverbs 31 together and think about the idea of economics, or household management. What stands out to you about this woman in the passage?

Have a conversation about the role of money in your family of origin. Do you have similar or different assumptions? If they are different, what are some ways you can meet in the middle?

Discuss together which partner you think is more financially responsible.

PART 4
Undressing for Sex

Chapter 12
Undressing the Sexual Self

Chapter 13
Undressing for a Life of Sex

Chapter 14
Undressing for the Wedding Night

Undressing the Sexual Self

Let's talk about sex.
—Salt-N-Pepa

How beautiful and how delightful you are, My love, with all your charms!
—Song of Solomon 7:6

POETS AND THEOLOGIANS OF SEX

The ancient world saw no need for such a thing as "sex education" because every Tom, Dick, and Sally could witness the procreation of their sheep, cows, pigs, horses, and dogs. Life was lived in the almost constant presence of animals, and from children to adults pretty much everyone could figure out the process by which baby animals were made. This knowledge was common to humans so long as we lived on, or near to, farms. It was only when we began to distance ourselves from the animal kingdom that the need to formally educate one another on the principles of sexual intercourse arose.

Today, our first exposure to sex is from our friends at a very young age. Typically they know next to nothing, but perhaps they had an older brother or sister who filled them in, or saw a magazine or film they oughtn't to have seen, and now enjoy their expertise relative to your innocence. To fill in the gaps, sex-ed courses, prosecuted in schools by awkward teachers to even more awkward groups of students, are a very specialized affair. Middle school-aged children are exposed to mechanistic descriptions of genitalia, the process by which semen interacts with an egg, and instruction in the proper methods for condom use. Questions of the purpose of sex, or the value of humanity, or the role of relationship are left aside. Those are questions of value, and the state's interest, after all, is to ensure that you have been properly "educated" relative to sex so that you will do it "safely" (whatever that may mean).

We may learn the *mechanics* of sex from our sex-ed class or from whispered conversations with our friends, but the place where we most absorb the meaning, significance, value, and role of sex in human life is from pop culture. And nowhere do we derive this set of meanings more than from popular songs. So let's take Salt-N-Pepa's cue, and talk about sex, but let's talk more about its meaning than its mechanics. After all, we're oversaturated with mechanical information—what we need is an understanding of value. In this, it seems that pop culture teaches us roughly five kinds of things about the meaning and significance of sex—that it is a need, consensual play, an expression of worth, an expression of power, and a religious experience.

At the ground level, the world tells us that sex is an animalistic need, a simple manifestation of our animal nature. In Hot Chocolate's song "You Sexy Thing," the very sight of the woman excites this animalistic desire, giving promise to the answer of my deepest needs. Such desire derives from our apelike ancestors and is as much a part of our human life as is eating, drinking, and sleeping. It is a chemically originated instinct which occasionally requires scratching.

A second narrative of sex we receive from culture is that sex is simply a matter of consensual play. Rod Stewart seeks such consent in his well-known song "If You Want My Body." So long as two people agree, what's the harm? And what, more than simple agreement, is required for sexual play between a couple? Consent, after all, is king. And consenting adults should be free to do as they please so long as their freedom doesn't harm anyone else.

Culture also communicates to us that sex is a measure of your personal worth. In line with this, James Brown invites us to exhibit our status as a "Sexmachine" on the figurative dance floor. My value, in other words, is an encapsulation of my sexual identity. The better I can get up on the scene, the stronger will be my personal value as a sex machine. Similarly, a woman's value lies in her capacity to be lovable. In other words, when you are sexy, you are valued. Lyrics (many unprintable!) abound which stand solely upon their objectification of women's bodies, creating a nearly overwhelming message from popular culture to women.

Another subtle but pervasive value communicated by culture is that our sexual self is an expression of our power and empowerment. Robin Thicke sings his song "Blurred Lines," which appears to push beyond the metrics of simple consent. Instead, the sexual encounter is now an opportunity to see how far we might push one another to do and perform those actions we personally desire. Sex is a game played where one person expresses power over another *by means of* sexuality. It isn't just songs by men, but female artists also portray sexuality *as* empowerment. Sex, then, is power—power over the other sex, power in the sexual relationship, power to satisfy your desires.

Lastly, in a song like Bruno Mars's "Locked Out of Heaven," sex is viewed as a religious experience. It is the perfected experience of paradise—the garden of the gods—and it is attained chiefly through our sexual congress. What could be better? Or more significant? At the close of his song, Mars even prays for entry into this paradise. What a worshipful suggestion!

Animalistic Need, Consent, Personal Worth, Power, and Worship—these voices whisper to us in our cars and homes, quietly but powerfully forming our expectations and thoughts about the meaning, purpose, and significance of the sexual self. When we as Christians dare to challenge these assumptions, a sliding scale shifts from definition to definition. Sex is alternatively either meaningless (animal, consensual), or the embodiment of everything (religious, mystical). Challenge culture to reconsider its ethics, and it will respond by claiming that sex means nothing. Challenge it to restrain itself and it will cry that sex is a need—like water or air!

For people who have rejected God and God's vision for the world He made, there is no higher joy or pleasure than sexual intercourse, and consequently no virtue in restraint. Malcolm Muggeridge, journalist and critic of Western civilization, writes that "Sex is the only mysticism offered by materialism." If this world is all there is, sex is the only transcendent remaining. Muggeridge continues, describing this materialistic congress further: "Sex pure and undefiled; without the burden of procreation, or even, ultimately, of love or identity. Just sex; jointly attained, or solitary—derived from visions, drug-infused; from spectacles, on film or glossy paper."[66] Today, the triple promises made by birth control, condoms, and abortion-on-demand assure us that sex is an activity devoid of all moral, human, or ethical consequences, and labors to maintain our illusion that it means both nothing and everything at exactly the same time.

INTO THE GARDEN—CHRISTIAN SEX-ED

It should be obvious that this is not the Christian ethic. And yet genuine Christian thoughts about the role of the sexual self are often buried in silence, distraction, and a dominating "no." Our silence is grounded in the fact that as Christians we have failed to reflect and to speak clearly about what it means to be a sexual being made in God's image. The distraction is in how we speak as if the only value of sex is the procreation of children. In this, we reduce physical intimacy to mechanics alone, and deny that there is real pleasure to be found and experienced in sex. And the word "No" dominates because, when we *have* spoken, the word that echoes loudest is a refusal: Don't touch. Don't look. Don't think. In thus failing to guide and shape the sexual self, we have helped to create the conditions where the voice of culture alone dominates and shapes the sexual conversation. Where we haven't spoken, the world has spoken on our behalf.

The Bible is far from silent on the question of sex, although many people, it would seem, imagine that the "don't speak" rule derives from Scripture. And yet Scripture is replete with the language and images of sexuality. Let's play a little game for a moment. Right now, whatever you do, *don't* think of a pink elephant with a purple bow. Seriously, *don't* think of a pink elephant with a purple bow. Be honest—were you able to avoid the thought? Or did it emerge unbidden into your mind? Rare people may be able to resist, but most people generate such images without a second thought—it's the nature of language to signal images to our minds in association with words. Now, read the following words from the Song of Solomon 4:5—"Your two breasts are like two fawns." Given the nature of language, are you really able to avoid thinking of breasts?

In the Bible sex is an acknowledged reality in language as well as the life of humans. In fact, one whole book of the Bible is dedicated to the subject of romantic love. The Song of Solomon, nestled quietly and safely in our Old Testaments, is an extended set of biblical song lyrics about love and sex (and contains some surprisingly erotic imagery!). Consider Solomon's words—words from the wisest man who ever lived—from Song of Solomon 5:1:

> I have come into my garden, my sister, my bride;
> I have gathered my myrrh along with my balsam.
> I have eaten my honeycomb and my honey;
> I have drunk my wine and my milk.
> Eat, friends;
> Drink and imbibe deeply, O lovers.

"I have come into my garden." With romantic love and sex in view, it is no surprise that the Song of Solomon compares the act of sexual intercourse to a garden, because in the ancient world the idea of a garden was commonly linked to the idea of sex. In Greek, the word for garden is *paradeisos*—what we in English translate as paradise. That word itself is made up of two Persian words that translate as a "walled enclosure." Walls created privacy, gardens offered delights. The heavenly delights of gardens were things meant to be protected—just like the act of sexual congress between a man and a woman.

The image of a garden provides us with a frame that can help us to understand how Christianity feels about the meaning and value of sexual intercourse. It is noteworthy to remember that the story of the Bible both begins and ends in a garden. In between, the story of God and His people begins with a kind of betrothal between God and Abraham. The betrothal becomes a covenant agreement at Sinai, which leads in time to John the Baptist, who acts as the "Friend of the bridegroom"—i.e., the best man. His job is to usher the bride (us) into the presence of the groom (Christ). In this story Christ's cross finalizes the wedding covenant, with the promised and much anticipated consummation happening at the great Wedding Supper of the Lamb. There, once and for all, God's people will dwell with God and enjoy the full benefits of His newly restored garden-paradise. In the interim, every human marriage is a miniature picture of God's covenant relationship with us, and every act of human sexual congress is a foretaste of the greater intimacy that is to come. The goodness of sex and orgasm is quite simply to be found in the fact that it really is a whiff of heaven. The significance we place upon our earthly sexual congress tethers out to the intimacy we are designed to experience with God. Sex, in other words, *is* very important, but its importance comes not from the act itself so much as from its deeper associations with intimacy and the consummation of our humanity. Sex, we believe, is not a need, and is not merely a matter of consent, does not measure our personal worth, is abused when used as empowerment, and is a false god when worshiped in itself. What it is, then, is a foretaste of the intimacy for which we are especially designed in the image of God. Such intimacy, we assert, belongs in a garden.

Consequently, we can draw from the image of the garden three properties that will help us to further understand our sexual selves in the light of God's image. A garden, after all, is walled, and cultivated, and enjoyed.

A GARDEN IS WALLED

Once again, the ancient word for garden, *paradeisos*, translates as "walled enclosure." It is a property of a garden that a wall sets a boundary on its perimeter, keeping the good in and the bad out, ensuring safety and pleasure for the inhabitants of the garden. Gardens are walled, and in the same way we place boundaries for our sexual perimeters to keep the good in and the bad out, and to ensure safety and pleasure for the garden's inhabitants. We might helpfully envision this wall in four different ways.

We can see this wall, first of all, as a wall of *appropriate time*. Three times in the Song of Solomon, at 2:7, 3:5, and 8:4, Solomon warns us with the following words,

> I adjure you, O daughters of Jerusalem,
> By the gazelles or by the hinds of the field,

That you do not arouse or awaken my love
Until she pleases.

There is an appropriate time and place for our expression of sexual love, and introducing it too early into life, and into a relationship, is dangerous. Inappropriate sexual timing wars against our capacity to develop intimacy at other levels of your life and relationship. It is an activity that short-circuits the required work of personal intimacy in a relationship—making a couple feel close and connected, but only superficially. It is very often, but not always, the man in the relationship who is most eager for sex. This is rooted in his hardwiring, which longs intensely (and often) to make love. If this part of his life is not under his control, then he is likely to push his girlfriend or fiancée to have sex. However, once this threshold is crossed he often becomes less interested or willing to cultivate other kinds of intimacy. For the woman, sexual intimacy is often an expression of emotional connection, and of a desire for greater connectedness between a couple. But outside the commitment of marriage, a woman will inevitably discover that the emotional intimacy she desired from offering herself in sexual intercourse did not result in deeper relational commitment. Such a situation creates the conditions for the woman to lose respect for both the man, and herself. Thus, outside of the timing of marriage, premature sexual intercourse awakens love before its appropriate time.

Another factor to consider is the role of the hormone oxytocin. When a woman gives birth to a baby, the doctors place the baby immediately at the mother's breast. A baby has limited vision—it can see about eight inches from the front of the face. This is, interestingly enough, just about the distance from the mother's breast to her face. When a mother breastfeeds, there is a chemical reaction in the bodies of both the baby and the mother—an exchange of oxytocin. This chemical creates a sensation of wellbeing and happiness, producing what some call a state in both babies and moms of being "milk drunk." We are hardwired, in other words, to love and in some ways become addicted to our children. This touches on our sexuality because oxytocin is released in our relationships as well—not only when we fall in love, or touch our beloved, but especially when we experience orgasm. This suggests, at a chemical level, that when we have sex we are training pathways of our brains to become addicted to the experience of our spouse. Awakening this reaction before its time plays with this reaction—we become chemically bonded to people *without* a covenantal commitment to protect and nurture that bond. It is dangerous to awaken such love before its time.

Lastly, if humans were *only* sexual beings—if culture is right and sex is an expression of a merely animal, instinctual need—then there would be no good reason to wait until marriage to experience sex with one another. If there were no other areas where development would be necessary for a successful marriage than the sexual, sex before marriage would seem like a great idea. To such a belief we offer the complexity of the whole human person—storied, of the heart, of the mind, of the soul, gendered, wounded, *personal*. To operate in life as if human beings are no more complicated than their sexual selves is to deny the complexity of our created nature in God's image. The unwillingness to wait—an attitude of impatience that drives early sexual union—not only cripples this growth in intimacy but betrays a weakness in character that may be destructive to the marriage later. Hence, we have a wall of appropriate time.

A second part of this garden wall is what we might call the wall of *sanctioned relationship*. Genesis 2:24–25 is again important, "For this reason a man shall leave his father and his mother, and be joined to his wife; and they shall become one flesh. And the man and his wife were both naked and were not ashamed." Those first words, "for this reason," point our attention back to the events we've just witnessed—to the creation of a special partner to walk with and be a helpmeet to Adam in his work. God has created man and woman so that man and woman will come together in God-blessed relationships, leaving their parents, and joining together to become one flesh. The "one flesh" of their union refers to three different things—to the mystical oneness of their marriage, to children created in the image of the parents (who are literally a single flesh made from two), and also to the act of sexual union. Marriage is the sanctioned relationship in which humans are intended to enjoy sexual congress together.

In this a good image to remember is that of the fire and fireplace. A fire is a great thing—it warms your house and cooks your food—but outside of the fireplace it is enormously dangerous, if not destructive. In the same way, sex is really good, but belongs in a specific place. Marriage is the fireplace where the fire of sex is safely burned.

The language of sanctioned relationship, in today's world, must be made further explicit. Any sexual activity that occurs outside the context of covenant marriage between a man and a woman is *unsanctioned*. This includes heavy petting, dry sex, manual sex, oral sex, anal sex, and any other kind of sex you can think of. It also excludes homosexual sex. All of these fall under Paul's injunction in 1 Corinthians 6:18 to "Flee sexual immorality." In Greek the word for sexual immorality is *porneia* and was used in the early church to clarify all sexual activity outside of marriage. Paul's reasons for this conviction become clear when we look at the rest of the passage:

> All things are lawful for me, but not all things are profitable. All things are lawful for me, but I will not be mastered by anything. Food is for the stomach and the stomach is for food, but God will do away with both of them. Yet the body is not for immorality, but for the Lord, and the Lord is for the body. Now God has not only raised the Lord, but will also raise us up through His power. Do you not know that your bodies are members of Christ? Shall I then take away the members of Christ and make them members of a prostitute? May it never be! Or do you not know that the one who joins himself to a prostitute is one body with her? For He says, "THE TWO SHALL BECOME ONE FLESH." But the one who joins himself to the Lord is one spirit with Him. Flee immorality. Every other sin that a man commits is outside the body, but the immoral man sins against his own body. Or do you not know that your body is a temple of the Holy Spirit who is in you, whom you have from God, and that you are not your own? For you have been bought with a price: therefore glorify God in your body.

We are cautious, in other words, with our sexual relationships because something beyond ourselves—beyond our momentary pleasures—is happening. Not only are we are being *joined*, and therefore playing as a game with God's gift and promise of heavenly intimacy, but we are spending our bodies as if they were our own. Your body is not your own, and the owner of your body has determined that sexual union is preserved for sanctioned relationships only.

A third part of this garden wall is the wall of *identity*. Walls, fundamentally, define spaces, and boundaries help us to discern meaning. With a wall we know where something begins, and where something else ends. Blurred or decayed boundaries invite lack of definition and confusion. When someone breaches a wall—such as in the case of a home invasion, or even a sexual assault—the real wounds are not physical so much as they are rooted in identity. Someone has trampled in and upon a sacred space. It is no surprise that in the Old Testament the apostasy of Israel is compared to the breaking down of such a wall. Isaiah 5:5 contains the following warning, "So now let Me tell you what I am going to do to My vineyard: I will remove its hedge and it will be consumed; I will break down its wall and it will become trampled ground." Israel's loss of their covenant protections with God results in a trampling of what was once a sacred space—the wall is removed, and Israel loses identity. Similarly, Ezekiel 16 contains a lengthy retelling of Israel's story, and prominent in that tale is the way that Israel's idolatry is envisioned as an act of prostitution. When the garden wall is removed, God's people lose their identity. When sexual boundaries are abolished, humans lose track of their sense of self. Thus, loss of sexual boundaries necessitates loss of personal identity, and the willful neglect of our sexual boundaries is a liberation that has the effect of diminishing our personhood.

To look at this another way, we might love to imagine a world in which we can copulate with any person we like, particularly any person with whom we feel deeply connected. But it seems also that in such a situation something within us would die. After all, when we analyze our desire for true intimacy it is far more textured; it cannot be reduced to the simply sexual. Our desire is to be truly naked and unashamed—naked historically, naked of heart, mind, soul, of gender, expectations, wounds, and all the rest. The sexual self is tied to every other part of your life, and when I permit myself to be reduced to my sexual self then those remaining capacities for intimacy die a little. This is, first, because when I am known by another human on a purely sexual level I am of necessity *not* known at any of those other levels. I am reduced, and my identity diminishes. But it is also because when identity is reduced to sexuality then relationships become utilitarian and controlling—your value to me is as a delivery system; you are only important to me because you can satisfy a particular desire. In such relationships neither person is maturing into the fullness of his or her humanity.

A fourth wall is the wall of *protection from danger*. Not only is sex reserved because of God's timing, and God's commands, and our sense of identity, but from specific dangers that transgression of the boundary can introduce to us. One image we can use to think about this helpfully is that of a shark-prevention net.

In 2005 Jeremy and Liesel took a trip to Hong Kong. While they were there, they visited a local island and snapped the following photo:

On the left of the frame, a helpful sign informs travelers of the importance of swimming within the boom line area. Clearly, on the ground, is the rope, leading to a buoy, to which is attached the boom line. A few feet further in is a second sign, slightly obscured, but which informs swimmers to "Keep Away from the Shark Prevention Net." The shark prevention net can also clearly be seen, stretching into the sea on the right. Now, while some signs and notifications are absurd and arbitrary, this, to us at least, seems like the kind of sign the average human who values his life and limbs would be eager to observe. Look once again at the picture, however, and you will note a man clearly swimming outside *both* the boom line area *and* the shark prevention net. There is indeed a word for this kind of person: shark food.

In the same way, couples who engage in sexual activity outside of the marriage covenant are swimming with sharks; they have ignored the wall of the garden that is designed to protect them. In doing this, we think they swim with five different sharks.

1. *The Shark of Shame.* Premarital sex introduces a number of shame-based issues into a relationship. The questions, for example, around the explanation of past partners are deeply awkward. The issues surrounding sexually transmitted diseases generate anxiety. In the event of an unwanted pregnancy, or even of an abortion, there is the shame that accompanies a story you would rather hide. For women, loss of virginity continues to be culturally considered a shameful thing—she is considered in some senses used, spoiled. (This, for the record, is an unjust double standard, because for men it is still considered a badge of manhood to lose your virginity.) The bottom line is that there is simply no such thing as "safe sex" apart from marriage.

2. *The Shark of Comparison.* A popular motto for travel to Las Vegas is that "What happens in Vegas stays in Vegas." But the truth of the matter (as one of Jeremy's friends once remarked), is that what happens in Vegas *stays in you*. In the same way, your past sexual experiences don't leave you behind, but travel with you into your future relationships, only to exert themselves upon your life-partner.

Women are already persons who regularly consider themselves *in comparison* to others—magazine covers, other women, and fashion—these are powerful factors. This competitive spirit is only magnified by comparing yourself to the other women your spouse has enjoyed sexually. Instead of intimacy, you will be wondering, "Am I as good? Do I look as nice? How did she do things?" Men also compare, but they compare their imaginations to reality. In this, men frequently compare their real, living wives to the imaginary and unreal women of pornography, mapping onto their spouses a set of expectations that no living woman can fulfill. These comparisons will wound your confidence and undercut your intimacy because they are forcing you to compare your experience when you ought to be enjoying your spouse.

3. *The Shark of Performance.* Watch commercials long enough and you will encounter pharmaceutical advertisements for products like Viagra and Cialis. The underlying assumption of these products is that if you, men, cannot maintain an erection then you are deficient. Your inability to perform is a mark against your manhood. Similarly, nearly every copy of *Cosmopolitan* magazine promises to reveal between 30–75 "Crazy-Hot Sex Moves" that will "blow his mind" on a monthly basis. The message, to you ladies, is that sex is chiefly about how you perform. If you are not sexually pleasing to your man—if you fail to put on the right moves—then you are essentially a relational failure. But the truth of the matter is that as soon as sex becomes performance it has been removed from the realm of relationship. Relationships—especially marriages—are about giving and taking, about connecting at the deepest possible levels, about succeeding and failing *together*. This means that a key component of marriage is that you are giving your spouse permission to fail. Thus, the undressing we do in marriage—the ability to be naked and unashamed—is the gift of being yourself without fear of examination. When sex becomes about performance, then we remove the honesty and safety provided by a covenant commitment that is necessary for couples to thrive.

4. The Shark of Dehumanization. Often when couples engage in premarital sex they excuse it by appealing to their perceived "need" for sex.
This, again, is a product of our culture's understanding of the sexual self.
In this view, sex is a need like other needs—when you're hungry, you
should eat; when thirsty, drink; when tired, sleep; when horny, screw.
But the absurdity of this becomes clear with a simple reflection: has
anyone ever died from a sex strike? Mahatma Gandhi once fasted from
food for twenty-one consecutive days in order to stop fighting and bring
peace to his native India. Imagine the absurdity if, at the outset of that
fast, he had declared to the Indian people "I will not have sex until you
stop fighting." It would have been laughable, because we understand
implicitly that sex is not the same kind of need as other desires. To prioritize it in that way is to make us no more and no better than animals,
to dehumanize us. When Jesus fasted forty days and nights, the devil
came to tempt him to turn stones into bread. Jesus answered by quoting
the Scripture, "MAN DOES NOT LIVE BY BREAD ALONE, BUT BY EVERY WORD
THAT COMES FROM THE MOUTH OF THE LORD" (Matt. 4:4). Note carefully
that Jesus said, not by bread *alone.* In other words, Jesus affirmed that
we humans are creatures made with both spiritual and material needs,
and that to give undue attention to the material needs in a critical way
dehumanizes us.

5. The Shark of Commodification/Objectification. We've already argued
that one of the key significances of sex is that it links us to the promised intimacy we will one day experience with God. What sex outside
of marriage can do is reduce this thing of great value to just another
commodity—a thing to be bought, sold, or traded. Sex can then
be used to gain influence, or power, or wealth. *The Georgia Straight,* a
Vancouver cultural newspaper, published in 2009 an article about pop
starlet Katy Perry that contained the lead line, "Katy Perry's career was
going nowhere until she wisely ditched Christian pop for songs about
girl-on-girl action."[67] In other words, Christian music wouldn't sell, but
sex did, and this was the inauguration of Perry's fame. Tragically, Perry
is now forced to ask herself if she is famous because she is talented, or

because she is sexually suggestive. The commodification of the value of her body must necessarily result in a question of her real value. In this, we place a wall around sex because we preserve its fundamental value, and we believe that men and women should be protected from objectification.

There's a good chance that, in reading this, you've been reminded of some place where you yourself have transgressed the garden wall of your sexuality. Ideally, you've already discussed these areas with your spouse (per your assignments during the lesson on undressing your stories). There may still be places that require confession, grieving, untethering, forgiveness, and repentance. Perform those actions as the need requires it, but please remember that the purpose of this chapter is positive and not negative—the goal is to give a clear picture of the Christian sexual self and to give a vision of what it might look like to embrace it more fully.

A GARDEN IS CULTIVATED

It is extremely important to clearly define the boundaries of sexual activity, but it equally important to stress that *protection* is an insufficient ethic to govern our sexual lives. Walls alone do not make a garden, because it must also be actively cultivated. Gardens, after all, don't just happen. Someone does the work to make a garden happen, to generate its own unique beauty, and that work takes the form of heavy investments of time, labor, planning, and patience. For the active cultivation of your own sexual self we think there are, broadly speaking, six kinds of methods you will use.

The first way we cultivate the garden of our sexual lives is through *commitment*, specifically, through commitment to one partner. It is a common myth that our sexual enjoyment increases with the number of partners we might have, as if the amount of experiences will correlate to a greater enjoyment of sex. However, in the same way that the best gardens are cultivated with dedicated attention to a specific space over a lengthy period of time, so the best sexual relationships are cultivated by a dedicated commitment to the man or woman you have married. Your commitment to your spouse, to the exclusion of all others, is a commitment to learning his or her unique desires, turn-ons, pleasures, and fantasies. No other woman or man can communicate what will please your spouse. Therefore it is only in commitment will you be able to access these depths and learn what it means to explore them together.

The second way we cultivate the garden of our sexual lives is through *intimacy*. This, in part, has been the summary argument of this whole book, that in marriage we are striving to once again be fully naked in the presence of another person and unashamed. Interestingly, the Bible has a few different words for when it refers to sexual intercourse. Genesis 4:1 tells us that Adam *knew* his wife Eve. The word "knew" is the Hebrew word *yada*, and in this case seems to marry intercourse with deep personal knowledge. The other word the Bible commonly uses is one we see in the superscript to Psalm 51, which tells us, mechanistically, that the Psalm follows the time that David "went into" Bathsheba. These two terms seem to separate sex into mechanistic and relational categories, between "just sex" and really making love. The invitation in Christian marriage, of course, is to know—to really *know* your spouse. That knowledge—when it extends to the whole person—will increase your sexual enjoyment.

Cultivation through intimacy ought to manifest itself in romance. After all, the very idea and practice of romance depends on this kind of knowledge—that you know, better than anyone else, what she or he likes. In romance you are communicating to your spouse a love that acknowledges his or her desires, preferences, and identity. As a result, in intimacy your nakedness will not be the nakedness of exhibition but of perfected vulnerability. Your intercourse will not be the mechanistic use of another person, but the joining of heart, mind, and body. So the rule is, quite simply, that if you want to experience great sex, get to know your partner.

Here a small warning is in order. The truth of the matter is that you can experience sexual arousal whenever there is an experience of deep connectedness between you and another person. Intimacy in one area can lead to a desire for intimacy in other areas. This reality stresses for us the importance of learning to restrain our sexual self—to know our boundaries, our hearts, and our desires, so that we will have the capacity to manage these impulses when we experience them. It also warns us against undue closeness with people of the opposite sex. An affair, after all, is almost never just about sex—you will cheat emotionally well before you cheat physically.

The third way we cultivate the garden of our sexual lives is through *visitation*. In 1 Corinthians 7:3–6 Paul gives advice to married individuals regarding the frequency of their sexual relationships:

> The husband must fulfill his duty to his wife, and likewise also the wife to her husband. The wife does not have authority over her own body, but the husband does; and likewise also the husband does not have authority over his own body, but the wife does. Stop depriving one another, except by agreement for a time, so that you may devote yourselves to prayer, and come together again so that Satan will not tempt you because of your lack of self-control. But this I say by way of concession, not of command.

A husband and wife, in other words, ought regularly to visit the garden of their sexual life together. We'll deal with the question of sexual frequency more specifically in the next chapter. For now, the main idea is that sex is cultivated in a couple by means of sex. You've got to practice, and practice regularly. This can lead to some concerns—can the husband demand sex on demand? Can the wife refuse? Clearly, in the metric of being one body in marriage—of the wife in a sense owning her husband's body, and the husband his wife's body—there is a call to mutual regard and respect. Sexual rights among Christian couples honor the person above all else as an image of God. You will have to agree together what frequency is right for you as a couple.

In this midst of this, there will be a gender-influenced temptation. For women, commonly you will want to prioritize intimacy over sex. Until you feel emotionally connected you won't strongly wish to make love. For men, the desire can become so pressing that you will prioritize the sex over intimacy. Until the urge is answered, you may struggle to draw close. There must be a place for both kinds of sex in a committed relationship—times when one spouse gives freely to the other, and times when one spouse commits to build intimacy as a bed for lovemaking.

The fourth way we cultivate the garden of our sexual lives is through *knowledge*. You don't know everything—far from it! And while you are forbidden to gain sexual experience with other partners, and while sometimes conversations about sexual technique are taboo, there are many suitable resources from which you can gain an education in the anatomy of sex and the varieties of pleasure that you can bring to one another. This book, and the chapter that follows this, aim to do precisely that. There may be a temptation to view pornography as a tool to increasing your knowledge and intimacy, but this is categorically a bad idea. Sex in pornography is entirely about performance; seeing other women and men have sex invites the shark of comparison into your marriage bed, and there are too many issues linking pornography use to addiction and harmful thoughts in men. Stay away from it! Flee immorality! Make sure, then, that your resources for sexual knowledge are not pornographic in nature.[68]

The fifth way we cultivate the garden of our sexual lives is through *developing our personhood*. The truth of the matter is that any two idiots can have sex. For the mechanical act, you don't *have* to know the person, you don't *have* to see them, you don't even *have* to be awake! But to make love to someone you *do* have to know them. And to get to know the person—to make it possible to make love to someone made in the image of God—then you both need to have a developed self that you can share with your partner. You've got to have interests, passions, loves, a history, and a life of your own. Without the development of your personhood, you bring little to the banquet of intimacy, and your sexual life will be shallow and untextured.

The sixth way we cultivate the garden of our sexual lives is through *caring for our bodies*. This is not an invitation to ape cultural standards, or to invite a layer of personal anxiety into your relationship, but merely to admit that our physical bodies are a critical aspect of sex act. Being fatigued, overweight, stressed, depressed, or injured are factors that can each become blocks to physical intimacy. In this, not only do we have an obligation to care for our own bodies (which are, after all, the property of our spouse!), but also to care for the body of our spouse as well. Ensuring that together you eat well, that there is sufficient time to exercise, and sufficient time to sleep, each of these things will increase your overall capacity to experience and enjoy sexual intimacy in the garden.

All gardens are cultivated, and to be enjoyed to the maximum benefit they are cultivated patiently and over time. We might note that while the first three tools—commitment, intimacy, and visitation—are tools of relationship, the second three tools—knowledge, personal development, and body life—are more technical. Given such complexity, it would be absurd to assume that a couple should be expert lovers on their wedding night. How could they, since they barely know one another, and barely know their bodies? Instead, the vision of the cultivated garden invites us to imagine our mutual cultivation as a lifelong process involving seasons of alternating planting and harvest—times of work, and times of play.

A GARDEN IS ENJOYED

Genesis 3:8 says that the Lord God, after He had made his garden creation, was walking in the garden in the cool of the day. The purpose of this garden, in other words, was so that it could be enjoyed. The garden of sex is similarly meant to be enjoyed—properly walled off, properly cultivated by two individuals in covenant relationship, they are then set free to enjoy the benefits of this garden.

We must never forget that God created sex. When He invented the world, sex was His specially designed plan for how new little humans would be made. It didn't *have* to be fun. It could have been carried out by a handshake, or a simple agreement and exchange of information.

Instead, we find that there are more nerve endings in human genitalia than any other part of the body. Why should that be, unless God wanted us also to enjoy the process? Why create a hormone that causes us to become attached, then addicted, to the man or woman we make love to? Why cause surges of hormones to drive us crazy with physical desire on a regular basis? Once again, God has designed sex, and that implies that each of these factors fall within His sovereign plan for our sexual life. This sacred garden, walled to protect its treasures, cultivated by men and women in commitment, is a place designed to be enjoyed. How you can enjoy it as a couple will be substantially the subject of the next chapter.

ASSIGNMENT . . . .

When did you first hear about sex? How do you remember that moment?

When did you first discover that your body could produce sexual pleasure?

Is it new to you to think of God's sexual design for us as a good thing? Either way, what impact do you think it ought to have on your relationship?

Very often, couples with sexual intimacy issues find that the real source of their struggle is in intimacy in other areas. How do you imagine cultivating those other areas with your spouse?

CHAPTER 13

Undressing for a Life of Sex

Fatigued as she had been by the morning's walk, they had no sooner dined than she set off again in quest of her former acquaintance, and the evening was spent in the satisfactions of an intercourse renewed after many years discontinuance.
—Jane Austen, *Pride and Prejudice*

"Everything is permissible," but not everything is beneficial.
—The apostle Paul

HEY! NO READING AHEAD!

Some of you, casually flipping through the pages of this book, have skipped ahead to the sex chapter, quite possibly in the quiet hope of peeking into what you think is the good stuff. If you're engaged and preparing for marriage, then stop right now! This chapter isn't for you yet. A central premise of this book is that sexual undressing is predicated on other kinds of undressing, that physical intimacy cannot be separated out from intimacy at every other level. The real good stuff of this book is found in all of the previous chapters, and this chapter is in many ways nothing more than icing on the cake. If you *are* married and are flipping through this book in the same way, well, then you ought to turn away as well. Occasionally men and women, feeling a strain on their marriage, hope that the addition of fresh sexual technique will resolve their issues with intimacy. This can only ever be little more than a patch to the real issues. Sexual intercourse is like the apex of a pyramid, which cannot stand if the foundations are not solid. The right order is to shore up the foundations of your intimacy, and then to that foundation add knowledge of sexual technique. To do things otherwise is to commit an injustice to your relationship.

If you're an engaged couple, we recommend that you wait to read this chapter until at least two weeks before your wedding date. There's no point titillating yourself too early before you can enjoy the benefits of your married life together.

With that out of the way, we can move on.

PERMISSION TO PLEASE

The garden of sexual delight, we have argued, is a place specially set apart for human pleasure—it is the walled and cultivated space within a marriage that is *made* to be enjoyed, to be enjoyed regularly, and to be enjoyed for a lifetime.

The question of pleasure may not sit as easily with some of you as with others. Many people commonly link the sin of the Garden of Eden to sex, presuming that "eating the forbidden fruit" was a euphemism for sexual intercourse. A closer reading of the text reveals that sex is nowhere mentioned in that chapter on the first sin. Instead, and quite explicitly, it is made clear that the original sin is made in an act of disobedience. It was not that the fruit had magic of its own—it was that God had asked us to abstain from it. By disobeying Him, we introduced sin into the world, and at its heart our own participation in sin is rooted in a deep disobedience of the heart. We sin, in other words, in exactly the same way as Adam and Eve. Altogether, then, there is no textual evidence to suggest that sex was the sin of Adam and Eve, and the fact that we have sometimes thought this to be the case might have more to do with our own fears than with God's design.

Additionally, you may feel that prioritizing pleasure in the marriage relationship is selfish. You may feel this especially if you are Catholic. For Catholics, intentional pursuit of the purely pleasurable aspects of the marriage relationship is suspect when separated from the ultimate purpose of procreation. The reality is, however, that couples are expected to have sex more often than the number of children they have. The apostle Paul, we read last chapter, even recommends regular sexual congress for the sake of sexual desire. Together, these factors suggest that pleasure—mutual pleasure—is a sanctioned product of a marriage relationship. It's okay to have fun with the wife (or husband) of your youth.[69]

Because sex is a matter of attention, and attentiveness, to the other—to your spouse—it stands to reason that masturbation sits outside of this ultimate purpose. The goal of sexual pleasure—and its height—is in the pleasure of another person. The goal of masturbation is in the pleasuring of yourself. Therefore we ought to set our attention on finding the best ways to please our spouse.

Song of Solomon 4:1–6 has a poem about the fun of sex, and includes some of the more erotic imagery!

> How beautiful you are, my darling,
> How beautiful you are!
> Your eyes are like doves behind your veil;
> Your hair is like a flock of goats
> That have descended from Mount Gilead.
> Your teeth are like a flock of newly shorn ewes
> That have come up from their washing,
> All of which bear twins,
> And not one among them has lost her young.
> Your lips are like a scarlet thread,
> And your mouth is lovely.
> Your temples are like a slice of a pomegranate
> Behind your veil.
> Your neck is like the tower of David,
> Built with rows of stones
> On which are hung a thousand shields,
> All the round shields of the mighty men.
> Your two breasts are like two fawns,
> Twins of a gazelle
> Which feed among the lilies.
> Until the cool of the day
> When the shadows flee away,

I will go my way to the mountain of myrrh
And to the hill of frankincense.

Hebrew poetry is all about repetition and association—the beauty of his bride's hair is compared to a flock of goats (because it is abundant?), all of her teeth are there (they "bear twins"), her neck is stately like a tower, and so forth. For our purposes, however, we should note that his descriptions of her beauty work from the top down—he begins with her hair, and moves down to her teeth, her mouth, her neck, her breasts. Then, in verse six, we find Solomon intending, during the cool of the day, to "Go my way to the mountain of myrrh, the hill of frankincense." The downward motion of his descriptions throughout the passage implies that Solomon is speaking here of this woman's most private parts, which would likely have been scented with myrrh and frankincense. And to think this was in your Bible the whole time!

This chapter is all about that fun—about foreplay, exploration, and intercourse, about learning to be the one great lover of your partner's life. It is about applying Solomon's wisdom to the marriage bed, in order to liberate us to be naked and unashamed in our sexual lives. In this chapter we hope to frame the sexual act from the perspective of maximizing the pleasure you can offer one another mutually within the boundaries of your marriage bed.

FOREPLAY

You've seen those pictures of icebergs where the camera is half underwater and half in the air—the pictures are astonishing. Above the water, we see only a small portion of this massive structure, when in fact almost 90 percent of its mass is submerged and invisible. In much the same way, the actual acts of sex are the 10 percent of your sexual life that are highly visible. Foreplay is the submerged 90 percent of the iceberg of sex. And foreplay, ironically enough, always begins with intercourse.

Consider, for example, the following sentence from Jane Austen's famous novel *Pride and Prejudice*—"Fatigued as she had been by the morning's walk, they had no sooner dined than she set off again in quest of her former acquaintance, and the evening was spent in the satisfactions of an intercourse renewed after many years discontinuance."[70] Did you do a double-take? They did *what* for the rest of the evening? If we don't know that "intercourse" refers, originally, to communication, then we will wonder about the quality of Mrs. Gardiner's character and choice of evening activities! In view of this, intercourse is a far more useful word than we give it credit to be. Not only does it refer (today) to our sexual union, but it also evokes this idea of an ongoing conversation. Thus, it captures key elements of relationship, of exchange, and of communication. The foundation of a life of pleasurable sex between you and your spouse will lie in your free exchange of ideas, because the only person who can tell you what feels good to your partner is your partner. No book, magazine, or friend can supplant your spouse for first-hand information on what is pleasurable. Therefore the first of the hallmarks of a healthy sexual relationship is ongoing intercourse—the ongoing conversation between a couple that allows for success as well as failure, for awkwardness, as well as growth.

To maintain this ongoing conversation, couples will do well to give priority to regard for one another. If, throughout the week, a husband is absentee, unhelpful, and unkind, then this will not facilitate receptivity to sexual union with his wife. If the wife is overcommitted, angry, and nagging, this will cause the sexual spark to wither. Sex begins long before your clothes come off—in small conversations, brief exchanges, and tiny kindnesses. If a wife *only* receives flowers from her husband when he is trying to romance her into bed, this communicates to her that his love is tied to her sexual favors.

Women, in point of fact, are very often like computer screens with many different windows open. They like to multitask, keeping a variety of projects active at the same time. One of the best ways that men can bid for their wives' attention—as an intentional act of foreplay—is to offer to close some of these windows for her. Perhaps she has a full agenda for the evening—to clean the kitchen, bathe the children, put them to bed, and finish a project. All of these windows are open at once, but you can offer to close several for her—you can volunteer to bathe and put the kids to sleep. In the meantime, she can focus her attention on other tasks and be fully present with you later.

Men are much simpler creatures. All that a woman has to do to arouse him, very often, is be in the same room. More pointedly, however, men are deeply visual creatures. The best foreplay for your husband will be to let him look at you. Getting dressed, or undressed, in his presence is a surefire way to capture and keep his sexual attention. Letting him watch you shower may drive him crazy. Adding lingerie to the mix will affix his attention even more, especially if you show it to him before you leave the house (which, be warned, may make you late to wherever you were going!). Lingerie is a funny thing, and you may feel that because you only wear it for a few minutes at a time that it isn't worth the expense. Check with your husband about his preferences—chances are, he thinks it's worth it!

Living in one another's presence—exhibiting kindness and regard for one another—can be sufficient foreplay to keep a sexual relationship fresh, and many couples may feel that they want all their sexual encounters to be spontaneous. However, in a marriage with work schedules, hobbies, volunteer work, and children, waiting for the spontaneous can be like waiting for a bus that will never arrive. Part of the foreplay game is also about planning and scheduling sexual activity together. You can reserve one day each week when you plan to get together for sex, and then still leave room for spontaneity on the other days. Knowing that sex is happening will help you to remember to be extra kind and show regard to one another that day. If you put sex in a shared calendar, you may want to use a code word to describe it, just in case someone else looks at the calendar. Pick a phrase you both agree on, "Baking," or "Blueberry Pie," or "Game Night." The code word can then serve as a signal to one another that you want to make love sometime soon. The wife can message her husband while he is at work with the promise of blueberry pie that evening, and he will hasten through whatever work he is doing to get home to her.

In addition to these activities, couples can also actively romance one another. "Romance" means different things to different people, so you'll have to work on your intercourse to find out what that is for your spouse. For some romance can mean gifts, like chocolate, flowers, or a meal. For others romance will mean a date, with a restaurant, conversation, wine, and a movie or a play. For others, romance will mean service, like doing laundry, the dishes, or fixing whatever needs fixing around the house. For still others, romance is children with the grandparents, candlelight, and a massage. For almost all couples, part of romance means cleaning, caring for, and preparing your body. Learn your spouse and romance him or her accordingly. Remember from our previous lesson that very often women require connection before sex, while occasionally men require sex for connection. Use your foreplay and romance to strike a balance between the two.

Lastly, kissing is probably the greatest foreplay activity of all. All of the other aspects of foreplay that we've mentioned so far have been mostly non-physical, but kissing is an intensely romantic engagement of bodies that acts as a prelude to sex. Lips are soft, and in connecting softness you can soften hearts and arouse passion. Open mouths become a tether to other opening parts of your bodies. Closeness brings faces, eyes, and smells into proximity, and the sheer pleasure of being so very *near* to another person can ignite intense longing and promising sexual fireworks.

EXPLORATION

If the 90 percent of foreplay is in order, then you are prepared for the remaining 10 percent of sex that is the subject of the rest of this chapter. It all begins with a process of exploration. Remember, fundamentally, that according to 1 Corinthians 7 your bodies *belong* to one another. Therefore in marriage you are given permission to explore one another, to see, touch, and taste the goodness of the person God has given you. The process ought to be pleasurable for both of you. As you explore, keep your intercourse up—ask questions—"How does this feel?" Give feedback, "Oooh! I like it!" Train one another in what is pleasurable.

The place to begin is by developing anatomical awareness together. Take time, together, to really learn one another's bodies. Look, touch, and explore one another's anatomy. Communicate clearly, taking cues regarding what feels good, and what doesn't. Wives, you will note immediately that your husband's erogenous zones are both external and focused on a specific area. Husbands, you will note that women are fundamentally different from you sexually—not simply because you have a penis and she has a vagina, but even more because you have a single erogenous zone (your genitals), but her whole body can be an erogenous zone. Brushing her hair, or touching the back of her neck, or the small of her back, or the area behind her knees, or the skin of her inner thighs, or massaging her feet—any of these sensations can bring her physical pleasure. Don't rush to what *you* think are her hot spots, because she can surprise you with her response to touch in other areas as well. Both of you will want to listen to one another regarding sensitivity, pleasure, and your level of arousal.

As you explore, you might pause to reflect on these biological differences for a moment. Why should it be that we are created by God with such stunning differences? Might it not be an opportunity for us to act out toward one another the high courtesy of heaven? In heaven's courtesy, Christ performs a mighty act, saying: "I offer my life for you." What if, in the marriage bed, the whole sexual act at some level exhibits this selfsame courtesy? Husbands, giving themselves to their wives, and wife to husband, a courteous, deep spirituality finding purchase in a sacred, erotic space.

Husbands, as you touch your wife's body don't fall into the trap of thinking that she's a machine that responds automatically with pleasure to your mechanized inputs. Sex therapist Lou Paget offers the following advice to men: "Women are like golf courses. Even though you may have played a course a hundred times, chances are your approach shot rarely lands in the same place on the green."[71] In other words, what worked on Tuesday may not work on Friday, so you'll have to pay attention, learn her body, and alter your approach based on the cues provided by her.

In the midst of this (brief) discussion of foreplay, we want to remind you of the apostle Paul's words from 1 Corinthians 6:12, "'Everything is permissible for me,' but not everything is beneficial." The first part of that sentence is the attitude of the Corinthians—they are acting on the presumption that in Christ their freedom makes everything permissible for them. And while they are right, Paul corrects their understanding with the words that, "not everything is beneficial." This is a good metric for regulating sexual freedom as well. In the marriage bed, between husband and wife in their sacred garden, everything really is permissible. But not all things will be beneficial—things that demean one spouse, or things that are abusive, or things that are painful, or things that one spouse really despises. In this, permissions are always regulated by benefits, and the benefits are determined by means of your intercourse as a couple. You've got to decide as a couple what you are comfortable with, discovering what is pleasurable and what is not. The key, of course, is to ensure that you are honoring your spouse.

Throughout this process, don't be a wet blanket to each other—don't just lay there and let your spouse work on you. Instead, give feedback—move, moan, talk, make noise. It's not a performance—it's *intercourse*.

INTERCOURSE

A significant part of the experience of foreplay is the physical preparation of the woman's body to receive the man inside her. However, not all bodies respond in the same way. As a result, it's a good idea to acquire some lubrication and keep it on hand. Popular brands like K-Y Jelly and Astroglide do well (avoid the fancy tingling or sensation-generating kinds until you've had time to explore one another more). Petroleum jelly is a no-go because you should never put it *inside* the body of your spouse.

When it comes to intercourse, there is simply no right or wrong way to do it—it all falls to the comfort and capacity of the couple.

The climax of the sex act, of course, is orgasm. Men, typically, get one shot at orgasm at a time. When young, they can recharge for orgasm in about 15–30 minutes. As they age, the recharge period can increase. Women, however, can experience orgasm again and again and again. Men, because they are driven to rush toward a big finish, often hurry the sex act along. But women, who are wired for the journey, can extend the lovemaking process out a lot further. If you're a young couple, early orgasm for the man shouldn't be too much of a problem. While he waits to recharge he can focus his attention on pleasuring his wife. By the time that she experiences orgasm, he will likely be ready again, and the pleasure can go on.

Orgasm feels different for men and women. As you experience orgasm together, take the time to discuss the sensations in your bodies—where you are affected, where you feel it, how you remember it, and how you feel afterwards. Remember, in your spouse you have access to a source of information otherwise completely opaque to you!

The movies make a big deal of couples seeming to experience orgasm at the same time. We hate to break it to you, but this is actually highly unusual, and it really isn't the most important value to consider while making love to your spouse. Most often one partner will experience orgasm before the other. If you are interested in pursuing mutual orgasm, you can research some of the techniques that men can use to either extend or delay their orgasms. We will refer you to other sources at the end of this chapter for learning this.

Lastly, the movies have lied to you in one, further, important way. In cinematic love scenes, after wild and passionate lovemaking, the couple regularly collapse side-by-side, falling asleep right then and there. What the movies don't tell you is that sex is often messy. We advise you to keep a small towel, some tissues, or a sanitary pad at hand to help clean up after sex.

HABITS FOR A LIFE OF SEX

It will be important, as you develop your sex life together, that you begin to develop some good habits for sex. You will first of all want to come to terms regarding the disparity between your sex drives.

Typically, women are ready for sex about once a week. Men, on the other hand, are ready for sex every two to three days. Clearly take time to discuss your expectations, and then make a plan to reconcile the differences with creativity. The good news is that not every session of lovemaking has to be an elaborate, mutually orgasmic experience. There are times for such elaborate lovemaking, but also times for casual, quicker sex. While the husband will not feel that he has had sex unless he has experienced orgasm, the wife may find that she can occasionally enjoy the closeness of sex without experiencing orgasm. Discussing your expectations will help you to decide what kind of sex you're having on a given day.

Although pain occasionally accompanies sex for women in their first encounters, for many women discomfort fades over time. But for some women, however, the pain remains. This pain can be caused by any number of circumstances, but you must understand that it doesn't have to be that way. Therefore if you find that you are experiencing ongoing pain in your sexual life, specifically through vaginal penetration, we strongly encourage you to see your physician and research treatment options. Sometimes a small change in lifestyle can bring relief. For other circumstances, additional treatments may be necessary. Either way, you don't have to live with pain in your sexual life.

The Bible, again, tells us that with regards to frequency, sex ought to happen fairly often in a marriage. Paul explicitly in 1 Corinthians 7 instructs husbands and wives *not* to deny one another. The only exception he offers is by mutual agreement for a time of prayer. So while there may be periods of absence, the healthy couple will ensure that they go to the garden with some regularity to enjoy its pleasures.

Once again, couples ought not to imagine that they will be expert lovers on their wedding night, and the reality is that growing well into a life of sex can take years. That's okay—you've *got* years. Commit to cultivating the garden, and the pleasures will increase over time.

ASSIGNMENT . . . .

If you're engaged, what part of sex are you most looking forward to? Are there parts of sex of which you are afraid? Discuss these together (but not too soon before the wedding night!).

If you're already married, did you take away anything new?

A NOTE ON RESOURCES

It is all too easy for books that educate couples on sex to veer into the pornographic and the simply crude. We have found that two of Lou Paget's books *How to Give Her Absolute Pleasure* (targeted for men) and *How to be a Great Lover* (for women) to be highly informative but not pornographic. Tasteful line drawings are both explicit and informative. Additionally, while Paget's books are not Christian books, she nevertheless prioritizes the role of relationship and of commitment to loving your partner in particular. These assets make it easy for us to recommend her books to you as an educational resource for your sexual lives.

Lou Paget, *How to Give Her Absolute Pleasure: Totally Explicit Techniques Every Woman Wants Her Man to Know* (New York: Broadway Books, 2000).

Lou Paget, *How to Be a Great Lover: Girlfriend-to-Girlfriend Totally Explicit Techniques That Will Blow His Mind* (New York: Broadway Books, 1999).

CHAPTER 14

Undressing for the Wedding Night

Vancouver! Vancouver! This is it!
—David Johnson, witnessing the eruption of Mount St. Helens.

EXPECTATIONS

The wedding night is an evening filled to the brim with expectations both spoken and unspoken. There is, on the part of the man, the promise of a real, live, naked woman. There is, for the woman, the promise of a new vulnerability. There is, for the man, a promise of orgasm. There can be, for the woman, a fear of pain. Each person may have expectations about how the evening will go, what kinds of things they will do together, and how the evening will end. Failing to undress these expectations can lead to frustration and disappointment.

When Jerry and Claudia were married nobody mentored them for the first night. Nobody talked them through it at all. What is more, at that time there were far fewer resources available than now. What little there was written by Christians about sex was too sketchy to be of any real use; and the material available from non-Christian sources was, to put it plainly, just raunchy. They wanted their wedding night to be full of passion and pleasure but knew far less than they were ready to admit. They felt the lack of good Christian material and didn't want the wedding night to be a time for sleaze. Nobody told them it was all right to talk about sex before they were married. And the lack of guidance on this matter reinforced the fact that sex was something to remain unmentionable. Somehow, on the wedding night, without guidance, without available resources, and being good Christians without practice and experience they were supposed to be naturals at making love. It was a set of expectations that did not set them up for success.

Dr. Kevin Leman tells the story of a young couple with vastly different expectations for their wedding night. When asked about his vision for the wedding night, the husband-to-be responded, "I just imagine myself waiting for her when she comes out of the bathroom in this beautiful, short, and I mean *really short* nightie, and underneath it she's got this little leopard-skin thong underwear." To this, the bride-to-be cries out in horror, "A *thong*? . . . You want me to wear a *leopard-skin thong*?!"[72] It's important to discuss what you think your wedding night will look like ahead of time. Are you staying in a hotel, or going home? Do you have a honeymoon suite, or a regular room? Are members of your wedding party "decorating" the space for you? If so, are they trustworthy people? Do you want candles, or flowers, or music? What kinds of clothing will you wear? All these kinds of questions ought to be asked well in advance of the wedding night itself.

Often, women believe that their first sexual experience on the wedding night will be unavoidably painful. Perhaps the most common reasons why a woman has a painful first experience with sex relates to her nervousness, the stress of the wedding, her lack of lubrication, and her husband's eagerness. If a woman, for whatever reason, is nervous about having sex she will most likely fail to produce vaginal fluids making it possible for her husband to enter her with ease. Consequently, if he in eagerness comes into her too soon it will be a cause of pain. No new husband ever wants to cause his wife discomfort, especially when it comes to sex, and especially if it will impact the future frequency of sexual intercourse.

A boy's eagerness for sex is tied to his hardwiring. At the time a boy reaches puberty all the bells and whistles of his sexual desire go off. If this happens when he is around twelve years old and he doesn't marry till he is twenty-two then he has had to wait for sex for ten years. It is difficult for a woman to know exactly how this feels for a young man. Perhaps these images might help: if sexual desire is an appetite, as some have suggested, it is as if a person has hungered for ten years before he can eat. If sexual desire is an instinct, as others have suggested, it is as if he has had an urge, like the urge to urinate, for ten years before he can relieve himself. Needless to say the drive is very strong. If a young man has sought to live responsibly so that he has avoided the utilitarian approach to sex some men value, then that young man on his wedding night is certainly operating at a high pitch of sexual desire. Furthermore this desire is made all the more intense by the looming possibility that the man will finally, after a lifetime fast, be able to take the edge off his desire. In this state, it is often the case that even the most well-meaning of husbands might cause pain to his wife on their wedding night. This is still a situation that can be avoided, but it requires awareness and intentionality.

Anyone who has read the account of the marriage night of the patriarch Jacob has certainly sensed something of the heightened tension of sexual desire implicit in the biblical text. Jacob had fallen in love with Rachel, the daughter of his uncle Laban. Required to pay a dowry so that he could marry his beloved, Laban required Jacob to work for seven years as an indentured servant. It is difficult to imagine the intensity of his desire, but the Bible story says that the seven years seemed but a few days for Jacob because of his love for Rachel. When the night of the wedding arrived Laban played a trick on Jacob, switching Rachel for her older sister Leah! We read that Jacob didn't discover the switch until the morning arrived. How was that possible? We can imagine that without light Jacob couldn't *see* Leah, or it might be that Jacob was inebriated from the wedding feast. But might it also not be that, after seven years, he was at such a high pitch of sexual desire that, having no reason to suspect a switch, he was hardly aware of the identity of the woman with whom he was having sex?

Claudia has said to Jerry often enough that if men didn't have such a strong sex drive they would be impossible to domesticate. They would always be out fishing with the guys, or playing sports, or cards, or doing something clubbable with other men, and talking about male matters. There may be something to this. Certainly no woman—even a bride— wants to think that a man's only interest in her is a sexual one. But a woman—especially a bride—would be living in denial if she thought a man wasn't sexually interested at all. These are simply the realities, and if a man has the volume turned up on his sexual drive on his wedding night and his bride is nervous there is likely to be pain involved.

THE STRESS OF THE WEDDING NIGHT

The truth of the matter is that your wedding night is probably the worst night of your life to start having sex. The accumulated stress of planning for a wedding sits on your shoulders. The memory of all the details that may or may not have gone well looms in your mind. Your body is exhausted from waking early, readying yourself, concluding final preparations, smiling, smiling, and smiling some more, troubleshooting whatever problems remains, answering Aunt Maude's irrelevant but important-to-her concerns, placating difficult relatives, not-eating, dancing, and whatever else has come up. Of all the nights to really relax and enjoy some sex, the wedding night ranks pretty near the very bottom.

The good news—and this may astonish you to hear—is that there really isn't a rule that says you *have* to have sex on your wedding night. You can wait until the next morning, after you've had some sleep, or you can wait until the next night, when you're away from all the mess. There's nothing beneficial to a husband in forcing his way into his wife's body if her body simply isn't ready to receive his penis. That doesn't mean you can't play together, and enjoy one another's bodies, and even orgasm together. But give yourselves time to de-stress before you force a situation that isn't necessary to force.

But chances are, you're still going to want to try. So how can a couple enjoy the pleasure of sex from the very first experience on the night of their wedding? Allow us to suggest a potential wedding night scenario—one that might make it possible for a bride to have a pleasurable experience rather than a painful one and a groom to feel more confident and patient rather than anxious and in a hurry.

First, remember your intercourse. The day of the wedding will be full of stress, so create the time and space to reconnect. Talk about the wedding, about how things went, about what went wrong and what went right. Talk about how beautiful your wife's dress is, how handsome your husband is. Hold hands, look into one another's eyes.

Second, restore your bodies a little. Couples at weddings very often don't get to eat. If this is the case, take some time for a meal or a snack. Go back to your hotel room and change into regular clothes, then slip back out to a restaurant and enjoy a meal together.

Third, try to relax. In your hotel room, while you are debriefing and enjoying one another, drink some wine together—not to get drunk, but to release the tension of the day. If wine isn't your thing, go for tea or hot chocolate. Take the time to massage one another. Take a bath together.

Fourth, go slowly. When you're ready to make love, begin small and be patient. Engage in foreplay with one another, exploring each other's bodies. When the time comes for you to attempt intercourse, try to make sure that your wife's body is ready to receive you. Go very slowly, and strive to minimize any discomfort. If there is pain, change tactics and try something else for a while.

Fifth, there is a high probability that the man, who has been looking forward to this night for so long, will experience premature ejaculation. He will be so excited to see his wife in all her glory, to be touched and kissed, that he will explode. This is okay. Turn your attention as a couple to the wife's body, and soon enough the husband will likely be ready to ejaculate again.

Jerry and Claudia were married in California. Their mid-day wedding was followed by a post-reception party at Claudia's parents' home. Leaving the festivities at around 7pm, they headed to their bridal suite, which Jerry had booked on the Queen Mary. By 7:30 Jerry carried Claudia over the threshold. The blood was pumping and the excitement about what was ahead was soaring—also the nervousness could not be hidden.

Jerry and Claudia's first date was at the Reef Restaurant in Long Beach, California. That night, instead of making love right away, Jerry and Claudia went out to eat together. There they talked about their wedding, about life, and reconnected with one another. When they got back to their honeymoon suite later that night, de-stressed and refocused on one another, they were able to make love without pain.

Jeremy and Liesel were married in Dallas, Texas (Jerry performed the ceremony). The wedding day itself was something of a disaster—many things went wrong visibly (with the exception of Jerry's part!). After leaving their reception at which they weren't able to sit and eat (because there was an oversight and no-one had set up a head table for them!) they drove to a nearby city and checked into their hotel. Starving, they changed clothes and headed to a nearby Italian restaurant where they waited, and waited, and waited for a table. Finally fed up with waiting, they walked to a different restaurant in the same parking lot, were seated immediately, but ate the most rubbery and tasteless meal of their lives. Returning to their hotel, exhausted, a little demoralized, and grumpy, they tried to make love but things simply weren't working. So they rolled over and fell immediately asleep, and that was their wedding night!

One couple succeeded, and the other failed—regardless, we're all still married today! The point in telling the stories is to help you remember that the wedding night, despite its hype, isn't everything. Your relationship together *is*. So on the night of your wedding, remember to take your time, love your spouse, and go as far as you can. You have the rest of your lives to enjoy together!

ASSIGNMENT ·

Separately, write down your expectations for your wedding night. Then trade papers and read one another's thoughts. Work to come to an agreement about how, generally, the evening together ought to go.

If you are already married, reminisce about your wedding night. What would you have done differently? What went well? If you could re-create the night, how would you make that happen?

PART 5

Final Words

Chapter 15
On the Writing of This Book

A Selected Bibliography of
Marriage Helps

On the Writing of This Book

The student is, or ought to be, a young man who is already beginning to follow learning for its own sake, and who attaches himself to an older student, not precisely to be taught, but to pick up what he can. From the very beginning the two ought to be fellow students. And that means they ought not to be thinking about each other but about the subject.
—C. S. Lewis

O n an unexpectedly warm and sunny day in December of 2003, I (Jeremy) stood next to Liesel in a church in Dallas, Texas, and was covenanted in marriage by my friend and mentor, Jerry Root. It was part of the beginning that made this book possible.

Some months previously, we had begun to meet, together with one other couple, at Jerry's house in the evenings to go through premarital counseling with him. The experience was enlivening. Jerry, as anyone will tell you who meets and speaks with him, exhibits a personality bursting with enthusiasm about Jesus, life, and experiencing God's blessings to the full. In those sessions, Jerry speaks without notes—after all, he has done premarital counseling for over a thousand couples, and his material has been extensively tried and tested. During those five sessions my bride-to-be and I—eager as we were—took extensive notes, listening, talking, and asking questions about Jerry's life. Graciously he never complained, but I'm sure we stayed late and kept him many times from other tasks that weighed on his agenda!

Those sessions were magical to begin with, and during the ensuing years of our marriage they have continued to bear fruit—shaping our thoughts and informing how we function in our marriage. Some years later, when I had become a pastor, it became my turn to offer Premarital

Counseling to a couple preparing for marriage. It was only natural that I would turn to our notes from our time with Jerry. From those notes and our memories my wife and I were able to reconstruct quite a bit, but there were still gaps, so at that point I reached out to Jerry and asked if he could share any further notes with me. Jerry shared that he and Claudia had worked on a book on Premarital Counseling together, and he graciously forwarded the draft with me. With the draft, and my own notes, I was able to fill in the pieces and offer a presentable product to the couples I was counseling.

Over the next several years I continued to counsel couples, and also began to write books. In conversation with Jerry, we wondered together if it might work for me to complete the draft of the counseling book he'd sent me. I was excited about the opportunity and agreed to undertake the project. It took a few years for me to get to it, but what you hold is the result of that work.

Describing what parts of the book are Jerry and Claudia's, and what parts I have contributed, is a somewhat impossible task. Jerry and Claudia's wisdom is the beating heart of the whole book, and it is a wisdom that I have sought to inhabit and live in my own marriage. The only other metaphor I could think of was of bones and flesh. The foundations of this book—its marrow, main ideas, or its bones, if you will—are Jerry and Claudia's, constructed from the forty-plus years of their marriage, and the near-countless couples they have encouraged and counseled in preparation for marriage. The product you now hold—the flesh, if you will—has been crafted through my own experience of living the material out in marriage and supplemented by my own work as a pastor in coaching couples in preparation for marriage. The metaphor is inadequate, but perhaps it will do.

A set of strong convictions motivates and gives life to this project. Chief of these is a heart of compassion for couples entering into married life. There is so much of marriage that brings us out of our depths and into a degree of both personal and interpersonal discomfort. We want to see couples equipped in the best possible means for a life of joyful marriage. This compassion was the very reason this material was developed in the first place—Jerry and Claudia wanted couples to have every advantage and felt that resources were lacking to offer such an advantage.

Extending from this compassion is a conviction that we carry about the importance of premarital counseling. Many churches require couples to seek some premarital counseling before a pastor will marry them, and this is a good practice. But couples, more than simply going through the routine, ought actively to seek to equip themselves for the future with as much energy and investment as is possible. In light of that, a book like this one can hopefully supplement a series of meetings with a pastor or counselor.

Premarital counseling is useful in more ways than one, however, because if you have gone to counseling *before* your marriage, then perhaps it will soften our common hostility to going to counseling *during* your marriage. In this, we are also convinced of the importance of counseling as a general practice. The message to couples is simply this—when you are in trouble, seek help. Don't be miserable, don't be unhappy, don't settle for life when things aren't working out. The thing is, with a marriage we get so stuck on our problems, and can get so rutted into habits of argument and response, that we forget how to see the big picture. A professional counselor can help us see those things and step out of those ruts. Many couples avoid counseling because of the cost, but this is a silly reason. If your roof leaked you would not hesitate to repair it so that you can live in a dry and comfortable home. Changing a roof costs tens of thousands of dollars; counseling will cost you only hundreds. Why not gladly spend the amount if it might result in living together in comfort?

However, more than cost, or shame, the most common reason that keeps people from counseling is pride. We are reminded of the story of Moses, Pharaoh, and the plague of frogs. In Egypt, a host of frogs had come out of the Nile and invaded Egyptian homes—beds, tables, cooking pots, frogs everywhere. Pharaoh, sick of the plague, finally summoned Moses. Their conversation is recorded in Exodus 8:8–11,

Then Pharaoh called for Moses and Aaron and said, "Entreat the Lord that He remove the frogs from me and from my people; and I will let the people go, that they may sacrifice to the Lord." Moses said to Pharaoh, "The honor is yours to tell me: when shall I entreat for you and your servants and your people, that the frogs be destroyed from you and your houses, that they may be left only in the Nile?"

Then he said, "Tomorrow." So he said, "May it be according to your word, that you may know that there is no one like the Lord our God. The frogs will depart from you and your houses and your servants and your people; they will be left only in the Nile."

Why does Pharaoh say "tomorrow"? Why, when he can that very night be free from frogs in his bed, his house, his kitchen, his favorite chair? The only reason to set a later time is pride. Sometimes, like Pharaoh, the fact that you must ask for help outside yourself can feel unbearable. Don't resist these resources! Give up your pride! Get the help! You'll be happier, and so will your spouse.

The argument of this book has been that a successful marriage is one that does the necessary work of marriage—to keep up the house, rake the leaves, and tend the garden—and that intimacy in marriage is a result of studied practice in all the areas discussed here. But it bears additional fruit as well. Jeremy, living with this material and putting it to practice, has found it formative of more than simply his marriage—marriage necessitates growth in empathy, and growth in empathy tethers out to every other relationship. Self-knowledge is cumulative. Growth in one area of spiritual fruit regularly leads to a harvest in other areas as well. In this respect, we believe that this book fills an additional and unique niche—in coaching couples for marriage, it also seeks to form their characters.

The end result, of course—and what might be the most important conviction of all—is that a good marriage is ultimately a testimony to Christ. Individuals who love one another sacrificially, forgivingly, committedly, who are being transformed by their contact with one another and their dependence upon Christ, are simultaneously testifying to the power of a God who commits to us, sacrifices for us, forgives us, and transforms us. All successful marriages are evangelistic in nature.

C. S. Lewis writes that the mature student's attention is less on the teacher than on the subject—that the successful educator is someone who has attached the student's interest in a lasting way onto the subject of their mutual study.[73] While this is, I hope, an accurate picture of how this book has come into being, it is our hope that something similar has happened as you read it. This is a book written under a set of specific convictions, chief of which is that marriages matter and that well-educated marriages have better opportunities for success. In this, your attention, as a couple, ought not to be on us as authors, or even on this book as a set of techniques, but to turn from these pages to your spouse—to regard, in a fresh and dedicated way—your marriage as a living, breathing thing that requires nurturing and attention to thrive.

May God grant that every couple who reads this book be blessed and enriched, to experience growth, encouragement, healing, and blessing, and to reach out in blessing to others. Amen.

A SELECTED BIBLIOGRAPHY
OF MARRIAGE HELPS

When I get a little money I buy books, and if any is left I buy food and clothing.
—Erasmus

The following selection of books is a sampling of resources that Jerry
and Jeremy have found especially beneficial. If you have taken up the
"book a year" challenge, you might begin with these.

On Marriage:

Briscoe, Stuart D. and Jill Briscoe. *Pulling Together When You're Pulled Apart*.
    Wheaton, IL: Victor Books, 1991.
Harley, Willard F. Jr. *His Needs Her Needs*. Grand Rapids, MI: Revell, 2011.
Mason, Mike. *The Mystery of Marriage*. Colorado Springs, CO:
    Multnomah, 2005.
Thomas, Gary. *Sacred Marriage*. Grand Rapids, MI: Zondervan, 2015.
Wangerin, Walter. *As for Me and My House*. Nashville: Thomas Nelson,
    1990.

On Love:

Chapman, Gary. *The Five Love Languages*. Chicago: Northfield, 1995.
Lewis, C. S. *The Four Loves*. San Francisco: HarperOne, 2017.

On Communication:

Gottman, John, and Joan DeClaire. *The Relationship Cure*. New York:
    Three Rivers Press, 2002.
Gottman, John, and Nan Silver. *The Seven Principles for Making Marriage
    Work*. New York: Three Rivers Press, 1999.

On Wounds:

Augsburger, David. *The Freedom of Forgiveness*. Chicago: Moody Press,
    1988.

Buechner, Frederick. *Telling Secrets*. San Francisco: HarperSanFrancisco, 2004.

Cloud, Henry. *Changes That Heal*. Grand Rapids, MI: Zondervan, 1992.

Nouwen, Henry. *Wounded Healer*. New York: Image Doubleday, 2010.

On Families and Expectations:

Cloud, Henry and John Townsend. *Boundaries*. Grand Rapids, MI: Zondervan, 2001.

Cloud, Henry and John Townsend. *Boundaries in Marriage*. Grand Rapids, MI: Zondervan, 2002.

On Parenting:

Thomas, Gary. *Sacred Parenting*. Grand Rapids, MI: Zondervan, 2017.

Tripp, Tedd. *Shepherding a Child's Heart*. Wapwallopen, PA: Shepherd Press, 2005.

On Sex:

Paget, Lou. *How to Be a Great Lover*. New York: Broadway Books, 1999.

Paget, Lou. *How to Give Her Absolute Pleasure*. New York: Broadway Books, 2000.

On Spirituality:

Lewis, C. S. Reflections on the Psalms. London: Geoffrey Bles, 1958.

Linn, Dennis, Sheila Fabricant Linn, and Michael Linn. *Sleeping with Bread*. Mahwah, NJ: Paulist Press, 1995.

Underhill, Evelyn. *Concerning the Inner Life: With the House of the Soul*. Eugene, OR: Wipf & Stock, 2004.

ACKNOWLEDGMENTS

Jerry and Claudia

There are many who should be acknowledged as people who, one way or another, contributed to the development of this book. Certainly, there are the over 900 couples I was privileged to marry, and some 600 couples more whose premarital counseling Claudia and I performed at that stage of their lives, helping them chart the trajectory for their marriages. There are, of course, too many to mention here, but we are grateful for every couple. And of course, there are many who must be acknowledged by name. We would like to acknowledge our children and their spouses: Jeremy and Michelle; Alicia and Zach; Grady and Leanne; and Jeff and Jori—each who married lovers of God, and have become good stewards of the gift God gave to each of them in allowing them to marry wonderful partners. Also, we personally thank Cassandra Sternthall, who walked us through some dark days in our own marriage and coached us in some life skills we had not yet acquired; giving us hope, and a light through the tunnel. We benefitted immeasurably from this therapist, endearingly called "St. Cassandra" by our family. Through her our children also learned not to be afraid when a need arises to go to the wise and get help. We must also acknowledge several others with whom ideas in this book were discussed over the years. There is Larry Fullerton, with whom Jerry served for a decade on staff at College Church in Wheaton. Together they set up the church's premarital counseling course. Furthermore, Jerry's writing group, *The Mead Men* (Lon Allison, Walter Hansen, Dave Henderson, the late Chris Mitchell, and Rick Richardson) gave valuable feedback. And, of course, we must acknowledge very close friends with whom life is full of deep reflection, engaging thought and discussion, all laced with good humor, wisdom, and sometimes mixed with tears. For Claudia it is her *Friends for the Journey* (Valerie Bell, Ginger Johnson, Cindy Judge, Darlene Hansen, Kristen Kriegbaum, and also her dear friend Cyndi McClure). For Jerry, those close friends with whom the ideas in this book were discussed, at some level, were: Professor Robert Bishop, David and Anne Brooks, Dr. Chris Claydon, Professor Jeff Davis, the late Professor Brett Foster, Pat Glasby, Professor Mark Lewis, Professor Dave Sveen, Dr. Tim Tremblay, and Professor Peter Walters.

Jeremy Rios

In many ways, Jerry and Claudia are the primary people I should like to acknowledge and honor here. Without their influence—and indeed, apart from the influence of the material in this very book—I doubt that I would be the husband, pastor, PhD student, or writer that I am today. In point of fact, my eldest son is named Moses *Root* Rios, a testimony to the nearly immeasurable influence that Jerry has had on my life. I also want to acknowledge my own wife, Liesel, without whom I would not be married at all, and with whom I have learned so much, and have so much more to learn. My children, Moses, Cates, Asa, and Lucy, privilege me with their insights, humor, and presence every day. She, and they, are as much a part of this book as I am.

NOTES

1   G. K. Chesterton, *What's Wrong with the World* (London: Cassell and Company, Limited: 1910), 254.

2   Billy Bray, *The King's Son* (London: Bible Christian Book-Room, 1874), 29.

3   Helmut Thielicke, *How the World Began: Man in the First Chapters of the Bible* (Cambridge, UK: James Clarke & Co., 1970), 99–101.

4   Song of Solomon 4:12–5:1.

5   Mike Mason, *The Mystery of Marriage* (Colorado Springs, CO: Multnomah, 2005), 61–62.

6   George MacDonald, *Unspoken Sermons* (Whitehorn, CA: Johannesen, 1997), 495.

7   Mason, *The Mystery of Marriage*, 46–47.

8   "Where there is no guidance the people fall, but in abundance of counselors there is victory" (Prov. 11:14.)

9   Lyle W. Dorsett and Marjorie Lamp Mead, eds., *C. S. Lewis: Letters to Children* (New York: Touchstone, 1995), 111.

10   See David Augsburger, *The Freedom of Forgiveness* (Chicago, IL: Moody Press, 1988), 144 and following.

11   Augsburger, *The Freedom of Forgiveness*, 16.

12   Edna St. Vincent Millay, "Baccalaureate Hymn" (*Vassar Quarterly*, Volume II, Number 4, 1 July 1917), 258.

13   Doug Liman, dir., *Mr. and Mrs. Smith* (Los Angeles: Fox, 2005).

14   William Wordsworth, *Wordsworth: Everyman's Selected Poems* (London: J.M. Dent, 1994), 305.

15   We will address some of these at greater length in the chapter on unpacking our woundedness.

16   G. K. Chesterton, *Orthodoxy* (Mineola, NY: Dover, 2004), 51.

17   G. K. Chesterton, *Tremendous Trifles* (Mineola, NY: Dover, 2007), 7.

18   There's more to say about this. All too often women marry men in the hope that they can change them into different people—they view their chosen spouse as a kind of project that they can mold in time to be or become something to her tastes. This is very bad logic, not only because it creates the conditions where you, the wife, adopt willingly the role of a nag, but because the more you strive to change your husband the more you are likely to diminish his sense of self. You think you are changing him, when in fact you are merely killing him in his innermost heart. A good rule of thumb is *not* to marry a man with whom you don't feel that you can partner.

210 NAKED AND UNASHAMED

19 Gary Chapman, *The Five Love Languages* (Chicago: Northfield, 1995).

20 This language is adopted from John Gottman and Nan Silver's work in *The Seven Principles for Making Marriage Work* (New York: Three Rivers Press, 1999).

21 C. S. Lewis, *Mere Christianity* (London: William Collins, 2012), 111.

22 http://www.today.com/popculture/jamie-lee-curtis-has-awesome-advice-staying-married-dont-get-t45481.

23 https://billygraham.org/decision-magazine/june-2013/ruth-bell-graham-a-life-well-lived-part-2/.

24 C. S. Lewis, *The Four Loves* (London: William Collins, 2012), 61.

25 For more on the role of rituals, including an extensive list of the kinds of questions couples can ask each other, see Gottman and Silver's *The Seven Principles for Making Marriage Work*, 251–253.

26 E. Stanley Jones, *The Christ of the Indian Road* (Nashville: Abingdon, 1926), 37.

27 Augustine, *Confessions*, Book I.

28 Corrie ten Boom, with Jamie Buckingham, *Tramp for the Lord* (Old Tappan, NJ: Revell, 1974), 55–57. The story of Corrie's time in Ravensbruck is told in *The Hiding Place*, one of the best Christian books ever written, and an eminently worthy read.

29 The *Examen* is also sometimes known as the Ignatian Exercises. A helpful (and playful) book on the exercises is called *Sleeping with Bread*, by Dennis Linn, Sheila Fabricant Linn, and Matthew Linn (Mahwah: Paulist Press, 1995).

30 Dorsett and Mead, *C. S. Lewis: Letters to Children*, 111.

31 Luke 2:19, 2:51.

32 William Shakespeare, *Poems* (New York: Alfred A. Knopf, 1994), 116.

33 Lewis, *Mere Christianity*, 113.

34 John Godfrey Saxe, *The Poems of John Godfrey Saxe* (Cambridge, UK: Cambridge University Press, 1868), 259–261.

35 William Wrigley, interviewed in *The American Magazine* in 1931. The article is entitled "Spunk Never Cost a Man a Job Worth Having."

36 C. S. Lewis, *An Experiment in Criticism* (Cambridge, UK: Cambridge University Press, 1961), 140.

37 Gottman and Silver, *The Seven Principles for Making Marriage Work*.

38 The categories in this section are adapted from Gottman's research. Please see his work for more extensive treatment.

39 Gottman and Silver, *The Seven Principles for Making Marriage Work*, 31.

40 Gwendolyn Green, ed. *Letters from Baron Friedrich von Hügel to a Niece* (Regnery: Chicago, 1955), 135.

41 John Gottman, *Why Marriages Succeed or Fail: And How You Can Make Yours Last* (New York: Simon and Schuster, 1994), 57ff.

42   John Gottman and Joan DeClaire, *The Relationship Cure* (New York: Three Rivers Press, 2002), 16.

43   Patrick Lencioni, *The Five Dysfunctions of a Team* (San Francisco: Jossey-Bass, 2002), 95.

44   Matthew 5:39.

45   Lewis, *An Experiment in Criticism*, 138.

46   Matthew 21:13, Luke 19:46.

47   In chapter one we discussed this process for forgiveness in greater detail.

48   The poem is Owen Barfield's, quoted from memory by C. S. Lewis in his *Letters to Malcolm: Chiefly on Prayer* (New York: HarperOne, 2017), 164.

49   Wordsworth, *Wordsworth: Everyman's Selected Poems*, 305.

50   Joel Porte, ed., *Emerson in His Journals* (Cambridge, MA: Belknap, 1984), 277.

51   Judith Wallerstein, Julia Lewis, and Sandra Blakeslee, *The Unexpected Legacy of Divorce: A 25 Year Landmark Study* (New York: Hyperion, 2000).

52   I (Jeremy) heard these questions during a personal conversation with Jim Houston.

53   Gus Van Sant, dir., *Good Will Hunting* (Santa Monica, CA: Miramax Films, 1997).

54   Lewis, *Mere Christianity*, 113.

55   Please note that we have slightly modified the Johari window for its application in marriage.

56   David W. Augsburger, *Pastoral Counseling Across Cultures* (Philadelphia: Westminster John Knox, 1986), 18.

57   Rudyard Kipling, *Kipling: Everyman's Library Pocket Poets* (New York: Random House, 2007), 52.

58   Augsburger, *Pastoral Counseling Across Cultures*, 18.

59   This language is borrowed from Rod Wilson, former president of Regent College and a licensed counselor.

60   Frederick Buechner, *Telling Secrets* (New York: HarperCollins, 1992), 10.

61   Thomas Fuller, quoted in Sherwood Eliot Wirt, ed., *Spiritual Disciplines: Devotional Writings from the Great Christian Leaders of the Seventeenth Century* (Wheaton, IL: Crossway Books, 1983), 31.

62   Evelyn Underhill, *Collected Papers of Evelyn Underhill* (London: Longmans, Green, and Co., 1946), 238.

63   See George E. Vaillant, *Triumphs of Experience* (Cambridge, MA: Harvard University Press, 2015).

64   Thomas Cathcart and Daniel Klein, *Plato and a Platypus Walk into a Bar* (New York: Penguin, 2008), 8.

65   When vetting a given organization to decide whether or not to include them in your charitable giving, it's a great idea to investigate the organization's efficiency. What percentage of the money you give will go toward operating

costs, and what percentage goes toward actually helping people? There are a variety of resources that can help you to find out these important numbers.

66 Malcolm Muggeridge, *Chronicles of Wasted Time* (Vancouver, BC: Regent College Publishing, 2006), 142.

67 *The Georgia Straight*, January 21, 2009, "Katy Perry's a Good Girl Gone Better."

68 For a few book recommendations, see the following chapter.

69 C. S. Lewis lends support to this view as well. He writes, "It has been widely held in the past, and is perhaps held by many unsophisticated people to-day, that the spiritual danger of Eros arises almost entirely from the carnal element within it; that Eros is 'noblest' or 'purest' when Venus is reduced to the minimum. The older moral theologians certainly seem to have thought that the danger we chiefly had to guard against in marriage was that of a soul-destroying surrender to the senses. It will be noticed, however, that this is not the Scriptural approach. St. Paul, dissuading his converts from marriage, says nothing about that side of the matter except to discourage prolonged abstinence from Venus. . . . With all due respect to the medieval guides, I cannot help remembering that they were all celibates, and probably did not know what Eros does to our sexuality; how, far from aggravating, he reduces the nagging and addictive character of mere appetite. And that not simply by satisfying it. Eros, without diminishing desire, makes abstinence easier." *The Four Loves* (New York: Harcourt, Brace and World, Inc., 1960), 136–140.

70 Jane Austen, *Pride and Prejudice*, (London: Penguin Books, 2003), 247.

71 Lou Paget, *How to Give Her Absolute Pleasure* (New York: Broadway Books, 2000), 5.

72 Kevin Leman, *Sheet Music: Uncovering the Secrets of Sexual Intimacy in Marriage* (Carol Stream, IL: Tyndale, 2008), 67.

73 C. S. Lewis, "Our English Syllabus," *Rehabilitations* (London: Oxford University Press, 1939), 85.

ABOUT PARACLETE PRESS

Who We Are

As the publishing arm of the Community of Jesus, Paraclete Press presents a full expression of Christian belief and practice—from Catholic to Evangelical, from Protestant to Orthodox, reflecting the ecumenical charism of the Community and its dedication to sacred music, the fine arts, and the written word. We publish books, recordings, sheet music, and DVDs that nourish the vibrant life of the church and its people.

What We Are Doing

Books

PARACLETE PRESS BOOKS show the richness and depth of what it means to be Christian. While Benedictine spirituality is at the heart of who we are and all that we do, our books reflect the Christian experience across many cultures, time periods, and houses of worship.

We have many series, including *Paraclete Essentials; Paraclete Fiction; Paraclete Giants;* and the new *The Essentials of...*, devoted to Christian classics. Others include *Voices from the Monastery* (men and women monastics writing about living a spiritual life today), *Active Prayer*, the award-winning *Paraclete Poetry*, and new for young readers: *The Pope's Cat*. We also specialize in gift books for children on the occasions of Baptism and First Communion, as well as other important times in a child's life, and books that bring creativity and liveliness to any adult spiritual life.

The MOUNT TABOR BOOKS series focuses on the arts and literature as well as liturgical worship and spirituality; it was created in conjunction with the Mount Tabor Ecumenical Centre for Art and Spirituality in Barga, Italy.

Music

The PARACLETE RECORDINGS label represents the internationally acclaimed choir *Gloriæ Dei Cantores*, the *Gloriæ Dei Cantores Schola*, and the other instrumental artists of the *Arts Empowering Life Foundation*.

Paraclete Press is the exclusive North American distributor for the Gregorian chant recordings from St. Peter's Abbey in Solesmes, France. Paraclete also carries all of the Solesmes chant publications for Mass and the Divine Office, as well as their academic research publications.

In addition, PARACLETE PRESS SHEET MUSIC publishes the work of today's finest composers of sacred choral music, annually reviewing over 1,000 works and releasing between 40 and 60 works for both choir and organ.

Video

Our DVDs offer spiritual help, healing, and biblical guidance for a broad range of life issues including grief and loss, marriage, forgiveness, facing death, understanding suicide, bullying, addictions, Alzheimer's, and Christian formation.

Learn more about us at our website:
www.paracletepress.com or phone us toll-free at 1.800.451.5006

SCAN
TO
READ
MORE

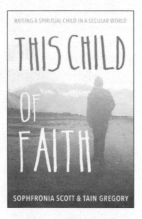